COMMUNICATION GAMES & ACTIV

SIDE by SIDE

THIRD EDITION

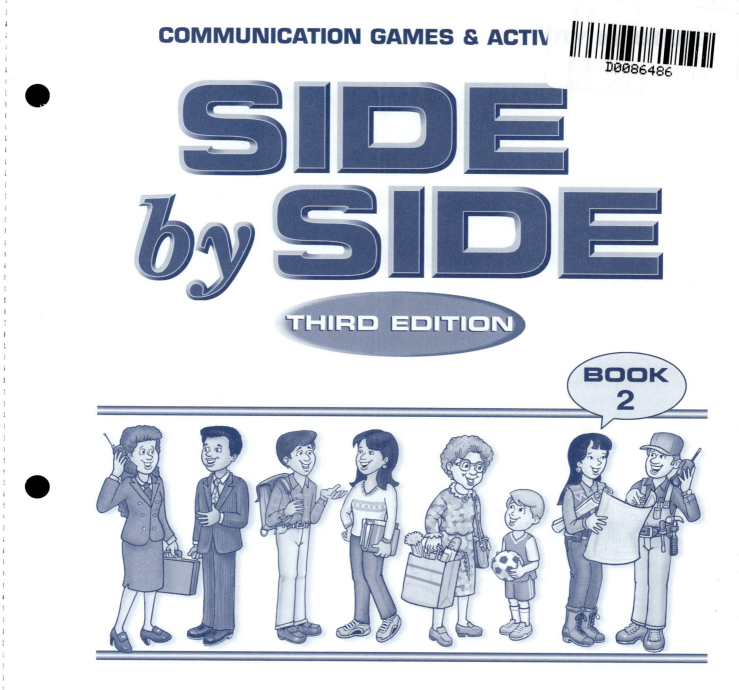

BOOK 2

Steven J. Molinsky
Bill Bliss

Contributing Author

Sarah Marlay

Illustrated by
Richard E. Hill

Longman

longman.com

Side by Side, 3rd edition
Communication Games & Activity Masters 2

Copyright © 2004 by Prentice Hall Regents
Addison Wesley Longman, Inc.
A Pearson Education Company.

Pearson Education, 10 Bank Street, White Plains, NY 10606

Editorial director: *Pam Fishman*
Vice president, director of design and production: *Rhea Banker*
Director of electronic production: *Aliza Greenblatt*
Production manager: *Ray Keating*
Director of manufacturing: *Patrice Fraccio*
Editorial supervisor: *Janet Johnston*
Associate art director: *Elizabeth Carlson*
Associate digital layout manager: *Paula D. Williams*
Digital layout specialist: *Lisa Ghiozzi*
Interior design: *Wendy Wolf, Lisa Ghiozzi*
Cover design: *Elizabeth Carlson*

Illustrator: *Richard E. Hill*

The authors gratefully acknowledge the contribution
of Tina Carver in the development of the original
Side by Side program.

Longman on the Web
Longman.com offers classroom activities, teaching tips and online resources for teachers of all levels
and students of all ages. Visit us for course-specific Companion Websites, our comprehensive online
catalog of all Longman titles, and access to all local Longman websites, offices, and contacts around the
world.

Join a global community of teachers and students at **Longman.com**.

ISBN 0-13-026767-8

2 3 4 5 6 7 8 9 10 – BAH – 05

Introduction

Side by Side Communication Games & Activity Masters 2 is intended to serve as a resource for dynamic, interactive activities to accompany Book 2 of the third edition of the *Side by Side* textbook series. These 64 activities, along with their accompanying reproducible activity masters, have been designed to reinforce the vocabulary and grammar structures presented in each chapter of the *Side by Side* text through pair, group, and full-class interaction.

Overview of Activity Types

The following types of activities are included:

Board Games—*group* activities in which students play a game that reviews key vocabulary and grammar structures through a variety of questions and tasks

Classroom Search Games—*full-class* activities in which students circulate around the classroom and ask their classmates questions

Group Discussion—*group* activities in which students discuss problem situations and then report back to the class

Group Projects—*group* activities in which students brainstorm ideas and then present them to the class

Guessing Games—*team* activities in which students make guesses based on verbal or visual clues

Information Gaps—*pair* activities in which students ask and answer questions in order to gain missing information

Interviews—*pair* activities in which students interview each other and then report back to the class about what they learned

Listening Games—*pair* activities in which students listen for information and then react or respond accordingly

Listening Grids—*full-class* activities in which students arrange visuals on a grid and then listen for clues that match the arrangement they have chosen

Matching Games—*full-class* and *group* activities in which students circulating around the classroom give verbal clues to each other in an attempt to find their appropriate "match"

Memory Games—*full-class* and *pair* activities in which students respond based on information they remember

Mystery Games—*group* and *pair* activities in which unknown answers to questions are revealed

Pair Discussion—*pair* activities in which students discuss questions and then report back to the class

Pantomime Games—*team* activities in which students respond to mimed actions

Pick-a-Card Games—*pair* activities in which students look for matches for cards they are holding

Picture Differences—*pair* activities in which students work together to identify differences in two pictures

Story Games—*pair* activities in which students ask and answer questions about stories in order to gain missing information

Team Competition—*team* activities in which students compete to answer questions

Tell-a-Story—*group* activities in which students write a story based on a set of visuals

Game Book Overview

The following are provided for each of the Communication Games:

- The activity type
- The corresponding *Side by Side* Student Book 2 pages
- The grouping arrangement—pairs, groups, teams, full-class
- The corresponding reproducible Activity Masters found at the back of the book
- A brief description of the activity
- A *Getting Ready* section with instructions for before-class preparation of materials needed for the activity
- Step-by-step instructions for doing the activity in class

The activities are intended to be done upon completion of the particular Student Book page. They may be used either before or after the Expansion Activities for each lesson suggested in the accompanying Teacher's Guide.

There are several strategies for pairing students for pair activities. You might want to pair students by ability, since students of similar ability might work more efficiently together than students of dissimilar ability. On the other hand, you might wish to pair a weaker student with a stronger one. The slower student benefits from this pairing, while the more advanced student strengthens his or her abilities by helping a partner.

We encourage you to modify or adapt these activities in any way you feel would be appropriate for your students. In keeping with the spirit of *Side by Side,* they are intended to provide students with a language-learning experience that is dynamic . . . interactive . . . and fun!

Steven J. Molinsky
Bill Bliss

Contents

Chapter	Side by Side Pages		Communication Games	Game Type	Game Book Page
1	2	1.1	What Do You Like to Do?	Classroom Search	1
	3	1.2	What Do They Like to Do?	Listening Grid	2
	4–5	1.3	The Mills Family Yesterday & Tomorrow	Listening Game	3
	7	1.4	Happy Birthday!	Story Game	4
2	11	2.1	Go Shopping!	Pick-a-Card	5
	12	2.2	The Foods in My Kitchen	Listening Game	6
	13	2.3	What's the Same & What's Different About These Kitchens?	Picture Differences	7
	13	2.4	The Foods at Amy's Party	Memory Game	8
	16	2.5	What Did You Buy at the Supermarket?	Matching Game	9
3	19	3.1	Foods I Need at the Supermarket	Listening Grid	10
	19	3.2	Go Shopping!	Pick-a-Card	11
	20	3.3	My Shopping List	Information Gap	12
	20	3.4	The Foods in Kevin's Kitchen	Memory Game	13
	21	3.5	Sam's Supermarket	Information Gap	14
	25	3.6	A Wonderful Dinner	Story Game	15
	25	3.7	The Food Game	Board Game	16
4	31	4.1	What's My Future?	Mystery Game	17
	31	4.2	Frieda, the Fortune Teller	Mystery Game	18
	33	4.3	Debbie Can't Decide	Information Gap	19
	33	4.4	I Can't Decide	Interview	20
	35	4.5	George, the Pessimist!	Story Game	21
5	40–41	5.1	Comparatively Speaking	Pair Discussion	22
	42–43	5.2	Let's Compare! Game	Board Game	23
	42–43	5.3	Which Do You Prefer?	Pair Discussion	24
	42–43	5.4	What Do You Think?	Interview	25
	45	5.5	Can You Remember?	Memory Game	26
	47	5.6	Good Advice	Group Discussion	27
6	51	6.1	Superlative Game	Board Game	28
	51	6.2	Ray and Roy: Two Very Different Brothers	Story Game	29
	56–57	6.3	Commercial Competition	Group Project	30
7	62	7.1	Good Directions!/Wrong Directions!	Matching Game	31
	63	7.2	How Do I Get There?	Information Gap	32
	64–65	7.3	Mystery Places	Listening Grid	33
	66	7.4	Let's Go by Bus!	Listening Game	34
	67	7.5	Getting Around Town Game	Board Game	35

Chapter	Side by Side Pages	Communication Games		Game Type	Game Book Page
8	72	8.1	The Best Secretary	Group Discussion	36
	72	8.2	How Well Do You Remember?	Memory Game	37
	72	8.3	How Do You Do Things?	Interview	38
	74	8.4	Everybody Complains About Howard	Story Game	39
	77	8.5	What's the Consequence?	Guessing Game	40
	79	8.6	Adverb & Conditional Game	Board Game	41
9	84	9.1	What Were You Doing?	Classroom Search	42
	84	9.2	Doing Different Things	Memory Game	43
	85	9.3	I Saw You Yesterday!	Matching Game	44
	88–89	9.4	What Happened to These People?	Memory Game	45
	90	9.5	A Very Bad Day!	Listening Grid	46
	90	9.6	Guess What Happened to Me!	Pantomime Game	47
10	95	10.1	Guess the Situation!	Guessing Game	48
	96	10.2	Frank and Tina: Two Unlucky People	Story Game	49
	98–99	10.3	Things They've Got to Do	Classroom Search	50
	101	10.4	Ability & Obligations Game	Board Game	51
11	106–107	11.1	A Complete Checkup	Listening Grid	52
	106–107	11.2	Medical Checkup Pantomime	Pantomime Game	53
	108–109	11.3	If You Want to Lose Weight	Team Competition	54
	111	11.4	Make the Rules!	Group Project	55
	112	11.5	We've Got Some Advice for You	Group Discussion	56
	113	11.6	Health & Advice Game	Board Game	57
12	116	12.1	What Will You Be Doing?	Classroom Search	58
	117	12.2	Betty's Busy Week	Information Gap	59
	119	12.3	Lots to Do Tomorrow!	Listening Game	60
	123	12.4	Future Continuous Game	Board Game	61
13	127	13.1	What Are the Differences?	Memory Game	62
	128–129	13.2	Bob's Bad Night!	Tell-a-Story	63
	130	13.3	Some & Any Question Game	Team Competition	64

Appendix

Activity Masters

Game Index

Communication Games

1.1  **What Do You Like to Do?**
CLASSROOM SEARCH   (Text page 2)

CLASS

ACTIVITY MASTER
1

The Activity

Students walk around the classroom asking each other what they like to do on the weekend.

Getting Ready

Students will do this activity as a class. Make a copy of Activity Master 1 *(Things I Like to Do)* for each student in the class.

❑ **1.** Give each student a copy of *Things I Like to Do.*

❑ **2.** Write the following conversation on the board and have students practice it:

> A. What do you like to do on the weekend?
> B. I like to watch TV.

❑ **3.** Have students walk around asking each other what they like to do on the weekend. When students have found someone who likes to do an activity on their grid, have the responding student write his or her name in that square of the grid. (Only one signature is necessary for each square.)

The student whose grid is filled with the most signatures is the winner of the game.

The Activity

Students fill in a grid with different verbs and listen to see if those verbs are used in sentences.

Getting Ready

Students will do this activity as a class. Make a copy of Activity Master 2 *(Listening Grid)* for each student in the class.

❏ **1.** Give each student a *Listening Grid*.

❏ **2.** Write the following verbs on the board:

cook	play	swim	write
cooks	plays	swims	writes
cooked	played	swam	wrote
cooking	playing	swimming	writing

❏ **3.** Tell students to choose nine of these verbs and write them in a different square on the grid.

❏ **4.** Next, call on individual students to say a sentence with one of the verbs on the board. For example:

Jane *played* the piano all afternoon yesterday.
Roger *swims* every day.
Mr. and Mrs. Jackson like to *cook*.

❏ **5.** If a student hears a verb that he or she has written on the grid, the student should put an X over that word.

❏ **6.** The first person to have three words with Xs in a straight line—either vertically, horizontally, or diagonally—wins the game. Have the winner call out the words to check accuracy.

The Activity

Students ask and answer questions in order to match what the members of the Mills family did yesterday and what they're going to do tomorrow.

Getting Ready

Make a copy of Activity Master 3 *(The Mills Family Schedule)* and Activity Master 4 *(The Mills Family Activities)* for each student. Cut each copy of Activity Master 4 into separate cards.

❑ **1.** Divide the class into pairs.

❑ **2.** Give each student a copy of *The Mills Family Schedule* and a set of *The Mills Family Activities* cards.

❑ **3.** Write the following question and answers on the board and have students practice saying them:

> A. Did Mr. Mills cook breakfast yesterday morning?
> B. Yes, he did.
>   No, he didn't.

❑ **4.** Student A decides what the members of the Mills family did yesterday and what they're going to do tomorrow, then puts the activity cards in the corresponding sections of his or her schedule.

❑ **5.** Student B asks Student A Yes/No questions about what is on Student A's schedule and arranges the Mills family activities on his or her copy of the schedule so they match Student A's version. For example:

> Did Mrs. Mills plant flowers yesterday?
> Is Mr. Mills going to write letters tomorrow?
> Did Timmy Mills go to the mall yesterday?

When students have completed the activity, have them compare schedules to make sure their activity cards are in the same places.

Option: When students have finished the activity, they can reverse roles and play again.

The Activity

Pairs of students ask each other questions to find information each of them is missing.

Getting Ready

Students will do this activity in pairs. Make copies of Activity Master 5 *(Happy Birthday! A)* for half the class and Activity Master 6 *(Happy Birthday! B)* for the other half of the class.

☐ **1.** Divide the class into pairs.

☐ **2.** Give a copy of *Happy Birthday! A* to one member of each pair and a copy of *Happy Birthday! B* to the other.

☐ **3.** Write the following questions on the board and have students practice saying them:

> What did he give her?
> What's he going to give her?
> What did she give him?
> What's she going to give him?
> What did they give him?
> What are they going to give him?
> What did they give her?
> What are they going to give her?
> What did they give them?
> What are they going to give them?

☐ **4.** Explain that each person has a paragraph with missing information. Students need to ask each other questions about the information that is missing and then write the information in the charts. For example:

Student A: What did Mr. Lane give his wife last year?
Student B: He gave her a bracelet.
Student A: Why did he give her a bracelet?
Student B: Because she likes jewelry.

☐ **5.** When students have completed the activity, have them look at their partner's paragraph to check their answers.

2.1 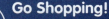 **Go Shopping!**
PICK-A-CARD (Text page 11)

The Activity

Pairs of students attempt to get rid of all their cards by finding matches for cards in their hands.

Getting Ready

Students will do this activity in pairs. Make two copies of Activity Master 7 *(Go Shopping! Cards)* for each pair. Cut each copy of Activity Master 7 into separate cards.

❏ **1.** Divide the class into pairs.

❏ **2.** *Give each pair two sets of Go Shopping! Cards.*

❏ **3.** Write the following questions and answers on the board and have students practice saying them:

A. Is there any *cheese*?	A. Are there any *apples*?
B. Yes, there is.	B. Yes, there are.
A. Is there any *cheese*?	A. Are there any *apples*?
B. Sorry, there isn't. Go shopping!	B. Sorry, there aren't. Go shopping!

❏ **4.** Have students shuffle the cards, take six cards each, and leave the remaining twenty cards in a pile. The pair should then decide which player will *go first.*

❏ **5.** Each player looks at his or her cards and puts any matching pairs in a pile face up. Player A must now attempt to find the match for the cards remaining in his or her hand. To do so, the player asks: "Is there any _____?" or "Are there any _____?" If Player B has that card, he or she responds: "Yes, there is" or "Yes, there are" and gives the card to Player A, who puts the matching cards in his or her pile. If Player B doesn't have the card, he or she tells Player A: "Sorry, there isn't. Go shopping!" or "Sorry, there aren't. Go shopping!" In that case, Player A must *go shopping* by picking a card from the pile. It is now Player B's turn to ask for a card.

The game continues until one player has no cards in his or her hand. The player with the most matching pairs wins the game.

The Activity

Students ask and answer questions in order to find out about the location of foods in a kitchen.

Getting Ready

Make a copy of Activity Master 8 *(My Kitchen)* and Activity Master 9 *(Food Cards)* for each student. Cut each copy of Activity Master 9 into separate cards.

❏ **1.** Divide the class into pairs.

❏ **2.** Give each student a copy of *My Kitchen* and a set of *Food Cards*.

❏ **3.** Write the following questions and answers on the board and have students practice saying them:

> A. Is there any bread on the counter?
> B. Yes, there is.
>   No, there isn't.
> A. Are there any lemons in the refrigerator?
> B. Yes, there are.
>   No, there aren't.

❏ **4.** Have each Student A choose eight food cards and put two in the cabinet, two on the counter, two in the freezer, and two in the refrigerator.

❏ **5.** Student B asks Yes/No questions about the locations of the foods in Student A's kitchen, then arranges his or her food cards so that they match Student A's kitchen.

When students have completed the activity, have them compare to make sure their food cards are in the same locations.

Option: When students have finished the activity, they can reverse roles and play again.

The Activity

Students ask questions about each other's kitchens to find similarities and differences.

Getting Ready

Students will do this activity in pairs. Make copies of Activity Master 10 (Kitchen A) for half the class and Activity Master 11 (Kitchen B) for the other half of the class.

❑ **1.** Divide the class into pairs.

❑ **2.** Give a copy of Kitchen A to one member of each pair and a copy of Kitchen B to the other.

❑ **3.** The goal of the game is for students to discover the following:

Two foods that aren't in Kitchen A, but are in Kitchen B
Two foods that aren't in Kitchen B, but are in Kitchen A
Two foods that are in both kitchens, but in different places

❑ **4.** The first pair to find the answer to these questions is the winner.

Answer Key

In Kitchen A, there isn't any pepper, and there aren't any tomatoes.
In Kitchen B, there isn't any soy sauce, and there aren't any oranges.

In Kitchen A, the carrots are on the counter and the flour is in the cabinet.
In Kitchen B, the carrots are in the refrigerator, and the flour is on the counter.

In Kitchen A, the bananas are in the refrigerator, and the potatoes are on the counter.
In Kitchen B, the bananas are on the counter, and the potatoes are in the cabinet.

The Activity

Students look at a scene with food items, then cover the scene and make a list of all the foods they remember seeing.

Getting Ready

Make a copy of Activity Master 12 (*The Foods at Amy's Party*) for each student.

❑ **1.** Tell students to take out a piece of blank paper.

❑ **2.** Give each student a copy of *The Foods at Amy's Party*.

❑ **3.** Tell the class that they have one minute to study the scene very carefully and then cover it with the piece of paper they had taken out.

❑ **4.** Have them make a list of all the food items they remember from the scene.

❑ **5.** The first student to correctly identify the 25 food items at Amy's party wins the game.

Answer Key

apples	french fries	lemonade	orange juice	salt
bananas	grapes	mayonnaise	pepper	sandwiches
cake	hamburgers	meatballs	pie	soda
cheese	ice cream	milk	pizza	spaghetti
cookies	ketchup	mustard	salad	tea

The Activity

Students tell what they bought at the supermarket in an attempt to find their match.

Getting Ready

There are 18 cards in this activity. You can do this as a class activity with 18 students, or you can divide your class into groups and use fewer cards to match the number of students in the groups.

Make two copies of Activity Master 13 *(A Little & A Few Match Cards)* for each group. Cut each copy of the Activity Master into separate cards.

❑ **1.** Give each student a different *Match Card*.

❑ **2.** Write the following conversation on the board and have students practice it:

> A. What did you buy at the supermarket?
> B. I bought a little rice and a few potatoes.
>   How about you?
> A. I bought a few lemons and a little cheese.
>   (or)
>   I also bought a little rice and a few potatoes!

❑ **3.** Two food items are depicted on each card. Based on their cards and using the conversation model on the board, have students walk around telling what they bought until they find their match.

❑ **4.** When all the students have found their matching partners, have them hold up their cards and tell what they bought. For example:

> We bought a little milk and a few potatoes.
> We bought a few eggs and a little butter.

3.1 **Foods I Need at the Supermarket**
LISTENING GRID (Text page 19)

CLASS

ACTIVITY MASTERS 2 & 14

The Activity

Students place pictures on a grid and then turn them over based on sentences they hear.

Getting Ready

Students will do this activity as a class. Make a copy of Activity Master 2 *(Listening Grid)* and Activity Master 14 *(Go Shopping! Cards)* for each student. Cut each copy of Activity Master 14 into separate cards.

❑ **1.** *Give each student a Listening Grid and a set of Go Shopping! Cards.*

❑ **2.** *Tell students to choose nine of the cards and place them on the grid, face up, in any order they wish.*

❑ **3.** *Say the following sentences in random order and tell students to turn over any card that you have described:*

> I need a can of soup.
> I need a jar of jam.
> I need a bottle of ketchup.
> I need a box of cereal.
> I need a bag of flour.
> I need a loaf of white bread.
> I need a loaf of whole wheat bread.
> I need a bunch of bananas.
> I need a head of lettuce.
> I need a dozen eggs.
> I need a pint of ice cream.
> I need a quart of orange juice.
> I need a gallon of milk.
> I need a pound of meat.
> I need a half pound of cheese.

❑ **4.** *The first person to have three turned-over cards in a straight line—either vertically, horizontally, or diagonally—wins the game. Have the winner call out the sentences to check accuracy.*

The Activity

Pairs of students attempt to get rid of all their cards by finding matches for cards in their hands.

Getting Ready

Students will do this activity in pairs. Make two copies of Activity Master 14 *(Go Shopping! Cards)* for each pair. Cut each copy of Activity Master 14 into separate cards.

❏ **1.** Divide the class into pairs.

❏ **2.** Give each pair two sets of *Go Shopping! Cards*.

❏ **3.** Write the following question and answers on the board and have students practice saying them:

> A. Do you have a can of soup?
> B. Yes, I do.
>   (or)
>   No, I don't. Go shopping!

❏ **4.** Have students shuffle the cards, take six cards each, and leave the remaining eighteen cards in a pile. The pair should then decide which player will *go* first.

❏ **5.** Each player looks at his or her cards and puts any matching pairs in a pile face up. Player A must now attempt to find the match for the cards remaining in his or her hand. To do so, the player asks: "Do you have a _____?" If Player B has that card, he or she responds: "Yes, I do" and gives the card to Player A, who puts the matching cards in his or her pile. If Player B doesn't have the card, he or she tells Player A: "No, I don't. Go shopping!" In that case, Player A must *go shopping* by picking a card from the pile. It is now Player B's turn to ask for a card.

The game continues until one player has no cards in his or her hand. The player with the most matching pairs wins the game.

The Activity

Students work together to find out what is on each other's shopping list.

Getting Ready

Students will do this activity in pairs. Make copies of Activity Master 15 *(Shopping List A)* for half the class and Activity Master 16 *(Shopping List B)* for the other half of the class.

❏ **1.** Divide the class into pairs.

❏ **2.** Give a copy of *Shopping List A* to one member of each pair and a copy of *Shopping List B* to the other.

❏ **3.** Tell students that the goal of the activity is to find out what foods are on each other's shopping list.

❏ **4.** Write the following conversations on the board and have students practice saying them:

> A. Do you need any bread?
> B. Yes, I do.
> A. How much do you need?
> B. One loaf.
> A. One loaf of bread?
> B. Yes, that's right.
>
> A. Do you need any bananas?
> B. Yes, I do.
> A. How many do you need?
> B. Two bunches.
> A. Two bunches of bananas?
> B. Yes, that's right.
>
> A. Do you need any cheese?
> B. No, I don't.

❏ **5.** Have the members of each pair take turns using these models to ask about what foods the other person needs. When a student has identified a food, that student should write it in his or her chart. For example:

> one jar of jam
> two bags of flour

❏ **6.** When the pairs have identified all the foods, have them compare their lists.

The Activity

Students look at a scene with food items, then cover the scene and make a list of all the foods they remember seeing.

Getting Ready

Make a copy of Activity Master 17 *(The Foods in Kevin's Kitchen)* for each student.

- ❏ **1.** Tell students to take out a piece of blank paper.
- ❏ **2.** Give each student a copy of *The Foods in Kevin's Kitchen.*
- ❏ **3.** Tell the class that they have one minute to study the scene very carefully and then cover it with the piece of paper they had taken out.
- ❏ **4.** Have them make a list of all the food items they remember from the scene.
- ❏ **5.** The first student to correctly identify the food items in Kevin's kitchen wins the game.

Answer Key

2 bunches of bananas	2 pints of ice cream	2 gallons of milk
a bunch of carrots	2 jars of jam	a quart of orange juice
2 boxes of cereal	a bottle of ketchup	3 cans of soup
a half pound of cheese	2 heads of lettuce	2 loaves of white bread
a dozen eggs	a jar of mayonnaise	a loaf of whole wheat
a bag of flour	3 pounds of meat	bread

The Activity

Students work together to determine the price of food at a supermarket.

Getting Ready

Students will do this activity in pairs. Make copies of Activity Master 18 *(Sam's Supermarket A)* for half the class and Activity Master 19 *(Sam's Supermarket B)* for the other half of the class.

❑ **1.** Divide the class into pairs.

❑ **2.** *Give a copy of Sam's Supermarket A to one member of each pair and a copy of Sam's Supermarket B to the other.*

❑ **3.** Write the following conversation on the board and have students practice saying it:

> A. How much does a quart of milk cost?
> B. Two nineteen.
> A. Two nineteen?
> B. Yes, that's right.

❑ **4.** Tell the class that they each have an advertisement for Sam's Supermarket. The advertisements are different, however. Student A knows the prices of food items that Student B doesn't know, and Student B knows the prices of food items that Student A doesn't know. Have the pairs ask each other questions to determine the prices that are missing in their ads.

❑ **5.** When the pairs have completed the activity, have them check their partner's advertisement to make sure they have written the correct prices.

The Activity

Pairs of students ask each other questions to find information each of them is missing.

Getting Ready

Students will do this activity in pairs. Make copies of Activity Master 20 (*A Wonderful Dinner A*) for half the class and Activity Master 21 (*A Wonderful Dinner B*) for the other half of the class.

❏ **1.** Divide the class into pairs.

❏ **2.** *Give a copy of A Wonderful Dinner A to one member of each pair and a copy of A Wonderful Dinner B to the other.*

❏ **3.** *Write the following conversation on the board and have students practice saying it:*

> A. What did John order for an appetizer?
> B. He ordered a bowl of chicken soup.
> A. How was it?
> B. It was delicious.

❏ **4.** Explain that each person has a paragraph with missing information. Students need to ask each other questions about the information that is missing and then write the information in the chart.

❏ **5.** When students have completed the activity, have them look at their partner's paragraph to check their answers.

The Activity

Students play a board game that focuses on food.

Getting Ready

Students will do this activity in groups. Make a copy of Activity Master 23 *(The Food Game)* for each group.

Each group will need a die. You can duplicate Activity Master 22 *(Game Cube)* to make a die for each group, or students can use a coin. Each player will also need a marker (a button or anything small) and a piece of paper.

❑   **1.**   Divide the class into small groups.

❑   **2.**   Give a copy of the *The Food Game* to each group. Also provide each group with a die, markers, and a piece of paper. If students use a coin as a die, the class should decide which side of the coin will indicate a move of one space and which will indicate a move of two spaces.

❑   **3.**   Have students place their markers on *Start*. The group should decide who goes first. That student begins the game by rolling the cube (or flipping the coin) and moving his or her marker. If the student responds to the question or task correctly, he or she may take one more turn. (The group decides if the response is correct.) If the student doesn't respond correctly, the next student takes a turn. No one may take more than two turns at a time.

Option 1: The first person to reach *Finish* is the winner.

Option 2: The game continues until each student reaches *Finish*. This way everybody is a winner.

4.1 What's My Future?
MYSTERY GAME (Text page 31)

GROUPS

The Activity

Students ask questions about their future and find out the answers by picking *magical mystery cards*.

Getting Ready

Students will do this activity in groups. Make a copy of Activity Master 24 *(Magical Mystery Cards)* for each group. Cut each copy of the Activity Master into separate cards.

❑ **1.** Divide the class into groups.

❑ **2.** Give each group a set of *Magical Mystery Cards,* and tell them to shuffle the cards and lay them face down in rows.

❑ **3.** Write the following on the board and check students' understanding:

Definitely!	100%	Probably not!	10%
Probably!	90%	Definitely not!	0%

❑ **4.** Have students take turns asking any question they wish beginning with "will" and picking a *mystery card* to discover the answer. For example:

Question	Card	Question	Card
Will I get married?	(Yes!)	Will I take a trip soon?	(Definitely!)
Will I win the lottery?	(No!)	Will I be famous?	(Probably not!)
Will I get a good job?	(Maybe!)	Will I become president?	(Definitely not!)
Will I become a doctor?	(Probably!)		

After students have each asked a question, have them take one or two additional turns, depending upon the size of the groups.

❑ **5.** When the activity is complete, have students take turns reporting to the class about a different member of their group. For example:

Carla will *get married.*
George won't *win the lottery.*
Maybe Thomas will *get a good job,* and maybe he won't.
Elena will probably *become a doctor.*
Michael will definitely *take a trip soon.*
Irene probably won't *be famous.*
Alan definitely won't *become president.*

The Activity

Students ask questions about their future and find out the answers from Frieda, the Fortune Teller.

Getting Ready

Students will do this activity in pairs. Make copies of Activity Master 25 *(Questions About My Future)* for half the class and Activity Master 26 *(Frieda, the Fortune Teller)* for the other half of the class.

❏ **1.** Divide the class into pairs.

❏ **2.** *Give a copy of Questions About My Future to one member of each pair and a copy of Frieda, the Fortune Teller to the other.*

❏ **3.** *Tell students that one member of each pair is Frieda, the Fortune Teller. The other person has questions to ask Frieda.*

❏ **4.** Have the students with questions about their future complete them on the Activity Master any way they wish. For example:

    1. When will _____ *I finish school* _____?
    2. How will I feel ____ *on my wedding day* ____?
    3. Who will _____ *be my best friend* _____?
    4. Where will _____ *I live in five years* _____?
    5. How many _____ *children will I have* _____?
    6. Will _____ *I be famous someday* _____?

❏ **5.** Have the students who are Frieda fill in the information on their Activity Master any way they wish. For example:

    1. a month and a year   *(January 2009)*
    2. an emotion   *(nervous)*
    3. a famous person   *(Tom Cruise)*
    4. a place somewhere in the world *(Rio de Janeiro)*
    5. a number between 1 and 20   *(15)*
    6. Yes, No, or Maybe   *(Maybe)*

❏ **6.** Have the pairs ask and answer their questions based on how they completed their Activity Masters, then call on pairs to present their questions and answers to the class.

❏ **7.** If you wish, *do the activity again and have students switch roles.*

The Activity

Students work together to figure out what Debbie might do each day of the week.

Getting Ready

Students will do this activity in pairs. Make copies of Activity Master 27 *(Debbie's Schedule A)* for half the class and Activity Master 28 *(Debbie's Schedule B)* for the other half of the class.

❏ **1.** Divide the class into pairs.

❏ **2.** Give a copy of *Debbie's Schedule A* to one member of each pair and a copy of *Debbie's Schedule B* to the other.

❏ **3.** Write the following on the board and have students practice it:

> She might play tennis, or she might ride her bicycle.
> She really can't decide.

❏ **4.** Tell the class that each person has different information about what Debbie might do each day of the week. The object of the activity is for each member of the pair to find out the missing information and write it in his or her copy of Debbie's schedule.

❏ **5.** When the pairs have completed the activity, have them tell the information that was missing from their schedule. For example:

Student B: On Monday she might go to the beach, or she might go to the park.

Student A: On Tuesday she might go to the gym, or she might go dancing.

The Activity

Students interview each other about things they're going to do and then report back to the class.

Getting Ready

Make a copy of Activity Master 29 *(Decisions! Decisions!)* for each student.

❑ **1.** Divide the class into pairs.

❑ **2.** Give each student a copy of *Decisions! Decisions!*

❑ **3.** Have students take turns interviewing each other, asking questions 1–6. Point out that there are four open-ended questions at the end. Students can ask each other any questions they wish. (Tell students to think of their open-ended questions and write them on the Activity Master before beginning their interviews.)

❑ **4.** Call on members of each pair to tell the class about their partners.

4.5  George, the Pessimist!
STORY GAME (Text page 35)

PAIRS

ACTIVITY MASTERS
30 & 31

The Activity

Pairs of students ask each other questions to find information each of them is missing.

Getting Ready

Students will do this activity in pairs. Make copies of Activity Master 30 *(George, the Pessimist! A)* for half the class and Activity Master 31 *(George, the Pessimist! B)* for the other half of the class.

❑ **1.** Divide the class into pairs.

❑ **2.** Give a copy of *George, the Pessimist! A* to one member of each pair and a copy of *George, the Pessimist! B* to the other.

❑ **3.** Write the following conversation on the board and have students practice it:

> A. Why are George's co-workers upset with him?
> B. He won't go to a restaurant with them tonight.
> A. Why not?
> B. He's afraid he might eat too much and get sick.

❑ **4.** Explain that each person has a paragraph with missing information. Students need to ask each other questions based on the model on the board about the information that is missing and then write the information in the charts.

❑ **5.** When students have completed the activity, have them look at their partner's paragraph to check their answers.

5.1 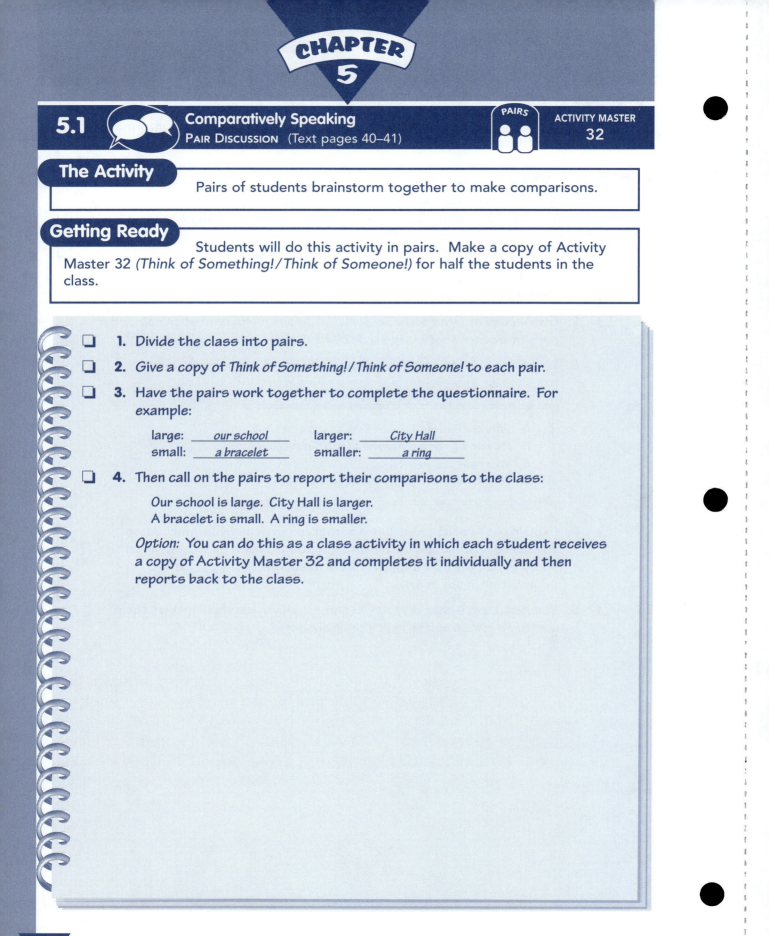 **Comparatively Speaking**
PAIR DISCUSSION (Text pages 40–41)

PAIRS

ACTIVITY MASTER
32

The Activity

Pairs of students brainstorm together to make comparisons.

Getting Ready

Students will do this activity in pairs. Make a copy of Activity Master 32 *(Think of Something!/Think of Someone!)* for half the students in the class.

☐ **1.** Divide the class into pairs.

☐ **2.** Give a copy of *Think of Something!/Think of Someone!* to each pair.

☐ **3.** Have the pairs work together to complete the questionnaire. For example:

large: <u>our school</u>   larger: <u>City Hall</u>
small: <u>a bracelet</u>   smaller: <u>a ring</u>

☐ **4.** Then call on the pairs to report their comparisons to the class:

Our school is large. City Hall is larger.
A bracelet is small. A ring is smaller.

Option: You can do this as a class activity in which each student receives a copy of Activity Master 32 and completes it individually and then reports back to the class.

5.2  **Let's Compare! Game**
BOARD GAME (Text pages 42–43)

GROUPS

ACTIVITY MASTERS
22, 33, 34

The Activity

Students play a board game that focuses on making comparisons.

Getting Ready

Students will do this activity in groups. Make a copy of Activity Master 33 *(Let's Compare! Game)* and Activity Master 34 *(Comparison Cube)* for each group. Make a cube from Activity Master 34 for each group.

Each group will need a die. You can duplicate Activity Master 22 *(Game Cube)* to make a die, or students can use a coin. Each player will also need a marker (a button or anything small).

❑ **1.** Divide the class into small groups.

❑ **2.** *Give a copy of the Let's Compare! Game and a Comparison Cube to each group. Also provide each group with a die and markers. If students use a coin as a die, the class should decide which side of the coin will indicate a move of one space and which will indicate a move of two spaces.*

❑ **3.** *Have students place their markers on Start. The group should decide who goes first. That student begins the game by rolling the cube (or flipping the coin) and moving his or her marker. When the student lands on a space, he or she rolls the Comparison Cube. If the cube lands on -er the student must make a statement using a comparative ending in -er—for example: "Peter is taller than Paul." If the cube lands on more, the student must make a statement using a comparative with more—for example: "Paul is more handsome than Peter." (The group decides if the response is grammatically correct.) If the student doesn't respond correctly, the next student takes a turn. No one may take more than two turns at a time.*

Option 1: The first person to reach Finish is the winner.

Option 2: The game continues until each student reaches Finish. This way everybody is a winner.

The Activity

Pairs of students state their preferences by making comparisons.

Getting Ready

Students will do this activity in pairs. Make a copy of Activity Master 35 *(Comparisons! Comparisons!)* for half the students in the class.

☐ **1.** Divide the class into pairs.

☐ **2.** Give a copy of *Comparisons! Comparisons!* to each pair.

☐ **3.** Have the pairs work together to decide which of the choices they prefer. For each of their choices, have them write 3 comparative sentences using any of the adjectives listed on the Activity Master. For example:

> We prefer a sedan. It's larger than a sports car. It's more convenient than a sports car. And it's cheaper than a sports car.

Option: You can do this as a class activity in which each student receives a copy of Activity Master 35 and completes it individually and then reports back to the class.

5.4  What Do You Think?
INTERVIEW (Text pages 42–43)

PAIRS

ACTIVITY MASTER
36

The Activity

Pairs of students interview each other and then report back to the class.

Getting Ready

Make a copy of Activity Master 36 (*My Classmate's Opinions*) for each student in the class.

- ❏ **1.** Divide the class into pairs.

- ❏ **2.** *Give a copy of My Classmate's Opinions to each student.*

- ❏ **3.** Have the pairs interview each other, asking the questions on the questionnaire and filling in their partner's answers. Point out that there are four open-ended questions at the end. Students can ask each other any questions they wish. Encourage students to give reasons for their answers. (Tell students to think of their open-ended questions and write them on the Activity Master before beginning their interviews.)

- ❏ **4.** Call on students to report to the class about their partners.

The Activity

Students look at pairs of pictures and try to remember the differences between them.

Getting Ready

Students will do this activity in pairs. Make copies of Activity Master 37 *(How Are They Different?)* and Activity Master 38 *(Memory Test)* for each pair.

❑ **1.** Divide the class into pairs.

❑ **2.** Give each pair a copy of *How Are They Different?*

❑ **3.** Tell students that they will have 3 minutes to study the pictures carefully and try to remember the differences—for example, Jane's office is cleaner than John's office. After they have studied the pictures, tell them to put the Activity Master aside.

❑ **4.** Next give each pair a copy of the *Memory Test*. Have them work together to answer the questions based on their memory of the pictures on Activity Master 37. In their answers, they should use *mine, his, hers, ours, theirs.* For example:

Question: What's the difference between Jane' office and John's office?
Answer: Hers is cleaner than his.

❑ **5.** When students have completed answering the questions, have them look at Activity Master 37 again to check their answers.

Answer Key

1. Hers is cleaner than his.
2. Mine is more powerful than theirs.
3. His is friendlier than hers.
4. Theirs is more comfortable than ours.
5. His is older than theirs.
6. Hers is prettier than ours.
7. Theirs is cuter than mine.
8. Hers is more delicious than his.
9. Theirs is bigger than ours.
10. Hers are better than his.
11. Mine is warmer than theirs.
12. His is more talkative than hers.

The Activity

Groups discuss solutions to problem situations.

Getting Ready

Students will do this activity in groups of three. Make a copy of Activity Master 39 *(Problem Situations)* for each group. Cut each copy of Activity Master 39 into separate cards.

❏ 1. Divide the class into groups of three.

❏ 2. Give each group a set of *Problem Situations* face down in a pile.

❏ 3. Before beginning the activity, review the expressions for agreeing and disagreeing presented in *How to Say It!* on *Side by Side* Student Text page 47.

❏ 4. Student A picks a card and reads the problem. Student B gives advice by telling Student A what the person with the problem *should do.* Student C listens and reacts to Student B's advice by agreeing, or disagreeing and offering a different solution to the problem. Then all three must discuss the situation until they reach agreement on what is the best advice.

❏ 5. For the next problem, Student B picks the card, Student C gives advice, and Student A reacts. Continue switching roles until all the problem situations have been discussed.

❏ 6. After the groups have finished their discussions, have them present their solutions to the class.

 **6.1** **Superlative Game**
BOARD GAME (Text page 51)

The Activity

Students play a board game that focuses on superlatives.

Getting Ready

Students will do this activity in groups. Make a copy of Activity Master 40 (*Superlative Game*), Activity Master 41 (*Superlative Question Cards*), Activity Master 42 (*Superlative Sentence Cards*), and Activity Master 43 (*Superlative Cube*) for each group. Cut each copy of Activity Master 41 and 42 into separate cards. Make a cube from Activity Master 43 for each group.

Each group will need a die. You can duplicate Activity Master 22 (*Game Cube*) to make a die for each group, or students can use a coin. Each player will also need a marker (a button or anything small).

☐ 1. Divide the class into small groups.

☐ 2. Give a copy of the *Superlative Game*, a *Superlative Game Cube*, and a set of *Superlative Question Cards* and *Superlative Sentence Cards* to each group. Also provide each group with a die and markers. If students use a coin as a die, the class should decide which side of the coin will indicate a move of one space and which will indicate a move of two spaces.

☐ 3. Have students place their markers on *Start*. The group should decide who goes first. That student begins the game by rolling the cube (or flipping the coin) and moving his or her marker. If the student responds to the question or task correctly, he or she may take one more turn. (The group decides if the response is correct.) If the student doesn't respond correctly, the next student takes a turn. No one may take more than two turns at a time.

Several of the spaces instruct the student to roll the *Superlative Cube*. When the cube is rolled, if it lands on *-est*, the student must make a statement using a superlative ending in *-est*—for example: "Ed is the nicest person I know." If the cube lands on *most*, the student must make a statement using a superlative with *most*—for example: "Jill is the most polite person I know." (The group decides if the response is grammatically correct.)

Option 1: The first person to reach *Finish* is the winner.

Option 2: The game continues until each student reaches *Finish*. This way everybody is a winner.

The Activity

Pairs of students ask each other questions to find information each of them is missing.

Getting Ready

Students will do this activity in pairs. Make copies of Activity Master 44 *(Ray Roberts & His Family A)* and Activity Master 45 *(Roy Roberts & His Family A)* for half the class and Activity Master 46 *(Ray Roberts & His Family B)* and Activity Master 47 *(Roy Roberts & His Family B)* for the other half of the class.

❏ **1.** Divide the class into pairs.

❏ **2.** Give a copy of *Ray Roberts & His Family A* and *Roy Roberts & His Family A* to one member of each pair and a copy of *Ray Roberts & His Family B* and *Roy Roberts & His Family B* to the other.

❏ **3.** Write the following questions on the board and have students practice saying them:

> Tell me about Ray Roberts.   What does everybody say about him?
> Tell me about Rachel.   What does Ray tell everybody?
> Tell me about Ron.   What do people say about her?
> Who likes Ray Roberts and   What do all the neighbors say?
>   his family?   What does everybody know?

❏ **4.** Explain that each person has two stories with missing information. Have students use questions like those on the board to discover information that is missing from their stories and then write the information in their chart. For example:

> Student A: Tell me about Ray Roberts.
> Student B: He's very nice.
> Student A: What does everybody say about him?
> Student B: Everybody says he's the nicest person they know.

❏ **5.** When students have completed the activity, have them look at their partners' paragraphs to check their answers.

The Activity

Groups of students create commercials using comparative and superlative adjectives.

Getting Ready

Students will do this activity in groups. Make a copy of Activity Master 48 (*Adjective List*) for each group and a copy of Activity Master 49 (*Commercial Cards*) for yourself. Cut Activity Master 49 into separate cards.

❑ 1. Divide the class into small groups.

❑ 2. Give a copy of the *Adjective List* to each group. Explain that the object of the game is for each group to create a commercial using as many comparative and superlative adjectives as they can. They should use the *Adjective List* as a reference for preparing their commercials.

❑ 3. Put the *Commercial Cards* in a pile face down on a table or desk in front of the room. To determine what each group's commercial will be about, have a member of each group come to the front of the room and select a card.

❑ 4. Allow the groups 15 minutes to prepare their commercials, then call on them to present their commercials to the class. Assign a different student in the class to be the *adjective counter* for each commercial. That person must listen carefully as the commercial is presented and count the number of comparative and superlative adjectives that are used. Assign another student to be the *adjective evaluator*. That person must listen carefully and decide if the comparatives and superlatives are grammatically correct and are appropriately used.

❑ 5. The group with the most grammatically correct and appropriately used comparatives and superlatives is the winner.

7.1  **Good Directions! / Wrong Directions!**
MATCHING GAME (Text page 62)

CLASS/
GROUPS

ACTIVITY MASTERS
50 & 51

The Activity

Students match directions and their corresponding maps.

Getting Ready

There are 20 cards in this activity. You can do this as a class activity with 20 students, or you can divide your class into groups and use fewer cards to match the number of students in the groups.

Make a copy of Activity Master 50 *(Main Street Directions)* and Activity Master 51 *(Main Street Maps)* for each group. Cut each copy of both Activity Masters into separate cards.

❑ **1.** Divide the class into groups.

❑ **2.** Give half the students in each group a *Main Street Directions* card and the other half a *Main Street Maps* card.

❑ **3.** Write the following sentences on the board, and have students practice saying them:

> Yes. Good directions!
> Sorry. Wrong directions!

❑ **4.** Have students circulate. Students with direction cards read their directions to students with map cards. If a map and directions card don't match, the student with the map responds, "Sorry. Wrong directions!" If a map and directions card do match, the student with the map responds, "Yes. Good directions!"

❑ **5.** When the pairs have found each other, have them read the directions and show the maps to the class.

The Activity

Students get directions from each other to places around town.

Getting Ready

Students will do this activity in pairs. Make copies of Activity Master 52 *(Downtown Map A)* for half the class and Activity Master 53 *(Downtown Map B)* for the other half of the class.

☐ **1.** Divide the class into pairs.

☐ **2.** Give a copy of *Downtown Map A* to one member of each pair and a copy of *Downtown Map B* to the other.

☐ **3.** Tell students that they know the locations of some of the places downtown and their partner knows the locations of other places. The object of the activity is for each of them to find out ways to get to places that aren't indicated on their maps.

☐ **4.** Write the following questions on the board and have students practice saying them:

> Excuse me. Can you tell me how to get to . . . ?
> Excuse me. Can you please tell me how to get to . . . ?
> Excuse me. Could you tell me how to get to . . . ?
> Excuse me. Could you please tell me how to get to . . . ?

Note: Point out to students that all directions start from the place marked with an X on their maps, at the intersection of Second Street and Tenth Avenue.

☐ **5.** Start the activity by having a student with Map A ask a student with Map B how to get to the shoe store. Student A can use any of the phrases on the board for asking for directions. In responding, Student B can use *next to, across from,* or *between*—depending on the particular location. For example:

A. Excuse me. Can you please tell me how to get to the shoe store from here?
B. Sure. Walk along Tenth Avenue and you'll see the shoe store on the left, next to the hotel/(or) across from the cafeteria.

☐ **6.** Continue the activity by having the members of each pair ask each other directions to places that aren't identified on their maps. When students find out the location of a place, they should write it on their maps.

☐ **7.** When the pairs have filled in their maps, have them check each other's map to make sure they wrote the correct names in the correct places.

The Activity

Students place the names of locations on a grid and then turn them over based on directions they hear to get to those places.

Getting Ready

Students will do this activity as a class. Make a copy of Activity Masters 2 *(Listening Grid)*, 54 *(Centerville Map)*, and 55 *(Mystery Places)* for each student. Cut each copy of Activity Master 55 into separate cards. Also, make a copy of Activity Master 56 *(Direction Cards)* and cut it into separate cards.

❏ **1.** Give each student a *Listening Grid*, a Centerville Map, and a set of *Mystery Places.*

❏ **2.** Tell students to choose nine of the *Mystery Places* and to put them on their grid, face up, in any order they wish.

❏ **3.** Read the *Direction Cards* in random order and tell students to look at the Centerville Map while listening to the directions, and when they hear directions to a *Mystery Place* on their grid, to turn that card over.

❏ **4.** The first person to have three turned-over cards in a straight line— either vertically, horizontally, or diagonally—wins the game. Have the winner call out the places to check accuracy.

The Activity

One student reads directions to places around town, and the other listens and writes the name of each place under the correct map.

Getting Ready

Make copies of Activity Master 57 *(Transportation Cards)* for half the class and Activity Master 58 *(Transportation Maps)* for the other half of the class. Cut each copy of Activity Master 57 into separate cards.

❑ **1.** Divide the class into pairs.

❑ **2.** Give Student A a set of *Transportation Cards* and Student B a copy of the *Transportation Maps*.

❑ **3.** Write on the board the following strategies for checking understanding and have students practice saying them:

> Did you say the First Avenue bus?
> Was that the Third Avenue bus?
> Did you say Fifth Avenue?
> Was that Sixth Avenue?
> Did you say "on the left"?
> Did you say "on the right"?

❑ **4.** Have Student A read the directions on the cards in random order. Student B listens and writes the name of the place under the correct map. Encourage Student B to check for understanding when necessary, using the types of questions on the board.

❑ **5.** When the pairs have completed the activity, have them compare the directions and the labeled maps.

❑ **6.** Then have students switch roles. Give each Student A a new copy of Activity Master 58. Student B reads the directions, and Student A listens and labels the maps.

The Activity

Students play a board game that focuses on getting around town.

Getting Ready

Students will do this activity in groups. Make a copy of Activity Master 59 *(Getting Around Town Game)* and Activity Master 60 *(Places Around Town Cards)* for each group. Cut each copy of Activity Master 60 into separate cards.

Each group will need a die. You can duplicate Activity Master 22 *(Game Cube)* to make a die for each group, or students can use a coin. Each player will also need a marker (a button or anything small).

❑ **1.** Divide the class into small groups.

❑ **2.** Give a copy of the *Getting Around Town Game* and a set of *Places Around Town Cards* to each group. Also provide each group with a die and markers. If students use a coin as a die, the class should decide which side of the coin will indicate a move of one space and which will indicate a move of two spaces.

❑ **3.** Have students place their markers on *Start*. The group should decide who goes first. That student begins the game by rolling the cube (or flipping the coin) and moving his or her marker. If the student responds to the question or task correctly, he or she may take one more turn. (The group decides if the response is correct.) If the student doesn't respond correctly, the next student takes a turn. No one may take more than two turns at a time.

Option 1: The first person to reach *Finish* is the winner.

Option 2: The game continues until each student reaches *Finish*. This way everybody is a winner.

8.1  **The Best Secretary**
GROUP DISCUSSION   (Text page 72)

GROUPS

ACTIVITY MASTER
61

The Activity

Groups evaluate five people to determine who would be the best secretary.

Getting Ready

Make a copy of Activity Master 61 *(The Best Secretary)* for each student in the class.

- ❑ **1.** Divide the class into groups.
- ❑ **2.** Give each student a copy of *The Best Secretary*.
- ❑ **3.** Tell students that these five people are applying for a job as a secretary. Each person does things differently. Each group should decide which person they think would be the best secretary based on that person's abilities and habits.
- ❑ **4.** After the groups have made their decisions, have them explain their reasons to the class.

The Activity

Students look at pairs of pictures and try to remember the differences between them.

Getting Ready

Students will do this activity in pairs. Make copies of Activity Master 62 *(Doing Things Differently)* and Activity Master 63 *(Do You Remember?)* for each pair.

❏ **1.** Divide the class into pairs.

❏ **2.** *Give each pair a copy of Doing Things Differently.*

❏ **3.** Tell students that they will have 3 minutes to study the pictures carefully and try to remember the differences—for example, *Julie speaks softly/Judy speaks loudly.* After they have studied the pictures, tell them to put the Activity Master aside.

❏ **4.** Next give each pair a copy of *Do You Remember?* Have them work together to circle the correct words and complete the statements based on their memory of the pictures on Activity Master 62.

❏ **5.** When students have completed answering the questions, have them look at Activity Master 62 again to check their answers.

Answer Key

1. can't / softly
2. can / loudly
3. isn't / carelessly
4. is / carefully
5. upset / impolitely
6. pleased / politely
7. is / early
8. isn't / late
9. Everybody / honestly
10. Nobody / dishonestly
11. careful / slowly
12. careless / fast
13. isn't / sloppily
14. is / neatly
15. isn't / awkwardly
16. is / gracefully

The Activity

Pairs of students interview each other about how they do various things.

Getting Ready

Students will do this activity in pairs. Make a copy of Activity Master 64 *(Rate Yourself!)* for each student in the class.

❏ 1. Divide the class into pairs.

❏ 2. Give a copy of *Rate Yourself!* to each student.

❏ 3. Have students answer the questions about themselves in Column 1, using any of the adverbs in the choice box.

❏ 4. Then have students talk with their partners. Before they tell their partners how they rated themselves, have the partners guess how the other person answered the questions.

❏ 5. Have students write their partners' guesses in Column 2 and compare their partners' answers with their own.

❏ 6. Have students report their answers and their partners' guesses to the class.

The Activity

Pairs of students ask each other questions to find information each of them is missing.

Getting Ready

Students will do this activity in pairs. Make copies of Activity Master 65 (*Everybody Complains About Howard A*) for half the class and Activity Master 66 (*Everybody Complains About Howard B*) for the other half of the class.

❑ 1. Divide the class into pairs.

❑ 2. Give a copy of *Everybody Complains About Howard A* to one member of each pair and a copy of *Everybody Complains About Howard B* to the other.

❑ 3. Write the following questions on the board and have students practice saying them:

> What does Howard's boss think?
> What does she tell him?

❑ 4. Explain that each person has a paragraph with missing information. Students need to ask each other questions about the information that is missing and then write the information in the chart. For example:

Student A: What does Howard's boss think?
Student B: She thinks he works too slowly.
Student A: What does she tell him?
Student B: She tells him he should work faster.

❑ 5. When students have completed the activity, have them look at their partners' paragraph to check their answers.

The Activity

Teams compete to guess how the rest of the class completed several statements.

Getting Ready

Make a copy of Activity Master 67 (*What Will Happen?/What Might Happen?*) for all but 6 students in the class. Also make a copy for yourself.

☐ 1. Ask for 6 volunteers. Divide them into two teams of 3 each, and ask them to leave the room for a while.

☐ 2. Give the remaining students a copy of *What Will Happen?/What Might Happen?*

☐ 3. Have them complete the statements any way they wish, using *will* or *might*. For example:

> If you go to bed too late tonight, you'll be tired in the morning.
> If you go to bed too late tonight, you might oversleep.
> If you go to bed too late tonight, you won't be able to get up on time.

☐ 4. One statement at a time, call on students to tell how they completed it. Make a tally of the 3 most frequent responses to each statement and write those on your copy of the Activity Master.

☐ 5. Call the teams back into the room. Tell them that they're going to hear statements completed by the rest of the students in the class and that they have to try to guess how the students responded.

☐ 6. Begin with Team 1. Read a statement from Activity Master 67 and have the team members talk with each other to agree on what they think the top response was from the class. Score as follows:

> A team gets 3 points if they guess response #1.
> A team gets 2 points if they guess response #2.
> A team gets 1 point if they guess response #3.
> A team gets no points if they don't guess any of the top 3 class responses.

☐ 7. Read a statement to Team 2. Continue to alternate statements between the teams. The team with the most points wins the game.

The Activity

Students play a board game that focuses on adverbs and conditionals.

Getting Ready

Students will do this activity in groups. Make a copy of Activity Master 68 (*Adverb & Conditional Game*), Activity Master 69 (*Consequence Cards*), and Activity Master 70 (*Action Cards*) for each group. Cut each copy of Activity Master 69 and Activity Master 70 into separate cards.

Each group will need a die. You can duplicate Activity Master 22 (*Game Cube*) to make a die for each group, or students can use a coin. Each player will also need a marker (a button or anything small).

❑ **1.** Divide the class into small groups.

❑ **2.** Give a copy of the *Adverb & Conditional Game* and a set of *Consequence Cards* and *Action Cards* to each group. Also provide each group with a die and markers. If students use a coin as a die, the class should decide which side of the coin will indicate a move of one space and which will indicate a move of two spaces.

❑ **3.** Have students place their markers on *Start*. The group should decide who goes first. That student begins the game by rolling the cube (or flipping the coin) and moving his or her marker. If the student responds to the question or task correctly, he or she may take one more turn. (The group decides if the response is correct.) If the student doesn't respond correctly, the next student takes a turn. No one may take more than two turns at a time.

Option 1: The first person to reach *Finish* is the winner.

Option 2: The game continues until each student reaches *Finish*. This way everybody is a winner.

9.1  **What Were You Doing?**
CLASSROOM SEARCH (Text page 84)

CLASS

ACTIVITY MASTER
71

The Activity

Students walk around the classroom asking each other what they were doing yesterday evening.

Getting Ready

Students will do this activity as a class. Make a copy of Activity Master 71 *(What Were You Doing?)* for each student in the class.

❏ **1.** Give a copy of *What Were You Doing?* to each student.

❏ **2.** Write the following on the board and have students practice saying it:

> What were you doing yesterday evening at 8 o'clock?

❏ **3.** Have students walk around asking each other the question on the board. When students have found someone who was doing an activity on their grids, the responding student should write his or her name in that square of the grid. (Only one signature is necessary for each square.)

❏ **4.** The first student whose grid is filled with signatures is the winner of the game. Have that student then report to the class about each of the activities. For example:

> George was watching TV.
> Angela was reading.
> Thomas and his brother were playing cards.

The Activity

Students look at two scenes and try to remember the differences between them.

Getting Ready

Students will do this activity in pairs. Make copies of Activity Master 72 *(They Were Doing Different Things)* and Activity Master 73 *(If I Remember Correctly)* for each pair.

❑ **1.** Divide the class into pairs.

❑ **2.** Give each pair a copy of *They Were Doing Different Things.*

❑ **3.** Tell students that they will have 3 minutes to study the pictures carefully and try to remember the differences between what Rob's family and Ron's family were doing yesterday afternoon—for example, Rob's mother was reading a book, and Ron's mother was reading the newspaper. After they have studied the pictures, tell them to put the Activity Master aside.

❑ **4.** Next give each pair a copy of *If I Remember Correctly.* Have them work together to complete the sentences based on their memory of the scenes on Activity Master 72.

❑ **5.** When students have finished completing the statements, have them look at Activity Master 72 again to check their answers.

Answer Key

1. Rob's mother was reading a book.
2. Ron's mother was reading the newspaper.
3. Rob's father was watching the news.
4. Ron's father was watching a game show.
5. Rob's older brother was ironing shirts.
6. Ron's older brother was ironing pants.
7. Rob's younger brother was playing the piano.
8. Ron's younger brother was playing the guitar.
9. Rob's older sister was doing her homework.
10. Ron's older sister was doing her exercises.
11. Rob's younger sister was listening to the radio.
12. Ron's younger sister was listening to CDs.
13. Rob's grandparents were baking a cake.
14. Ron's grandparents were baking cookies.
15. Rob's aunt was knitting a sweater.
16. Ron's aunt was knitting mittens.
17. Rob's uncle was eating a salad.
18. Ron's uncle was eating a sandwich.
19. Rob's cousins were playing soccer.
20. Ron's cousins were playing baseball.
21. Rob's neighbors were washing their windows.
22. Ron's neighbors were washing their car.
23. Rob was feeding his dog.
24. Ron was feeding his cat.

The Activity

Students look for the person who matches what someone was doing yesterday.

Getting Ready

There are 20 cards in this activity. You can do this as a class activity with 20 students, or you can divide your class into groups and use fewer cards to match the number of students in the groups.

Make two copies of Activity Master 74 *(Yesterday Match Cards)* for each group. Cut each Activity Master into separate cards.

❏ **1.** Give each student a different *Yesterday Match Card*.

❏ **2.** Write the following on the board:

> A. I saw you yesterday at 3 o'clock, but you didn't see me.
>   You were _____ing.
>
> B. That wasn't me. Yesterday at 3 o'clock I was _____ing.
>   (or)
>   You're right. I was!

❏ **3.** Have students walk around beginning a conversation with others using Line A and completing it based on the picture card they're holding. For example:

> I saw you yesterday at 3 o'clock, but you didn't see me.
> You were jogging through the park.

The other person responds based on the card he or she is holding. For example, if the card doesn't match, the person responds:

> That wasn't me. Yesterday at 3 o'clock I was rollerblading along Main Street.

If the other person is holding a card that matches, the person responds:

> You're right. I was!

❏ **4.** When all the students have found their matching partners, have them hold up their cards to show the complete matching version of each conversation.

The Activity

Students look at two scenes and try to remember what happened to people.

Getting Ready

Students will do this activity in pairs. Make a copy of Activity Master 75 (*What Happened to These People?*) and Activity Master 76 (*18 Unfortunate Things!*) for each pair.

❑ **1.** Divide the class into pairs.

❑ **2.** Give each pair a copy of *What Happened to These People?*

❑ **3.** Tell students that they have 3 minutes to study the pictures carefully and try to remember 18 unfortunate things that happened. For example:

Yesterday: A man hurt himself while he was fixing a door.
Today: A woman hurt herself while she was fixing a window.

After they have studied the pictures, tell them to put the Activity Master aside.

❑ **4.** Next give each pair a copy of *18 Unfortunate Things!* Have them work together to complete the information based on their memory of the scenes on Activity Master 75.

❑ **5.** When students have finished completing the information, have them look at Activity Master 75 again to check their answers.

Answer Key

Yesterday: A man hurt himself while he was fixing a door.
Today: A woman hurt herself while she was fixing a window.
Yesterday: A woman dropped her packages while she was walking out of the bank.
Today: A man dropped his packages while he was walking out of the bakery.
Yesterday: A man fainted while he was waiting for a taxi.
Today: A woman fainted while she was waiting for the bus.
Yesterday: A woman lost her purse while she was walking out of the supermarket.
Today: A man lost his wallet while he was jogging through the park.
Yesterday: A man got a flat tire while he was driving over a bridge.
Today: A woman got a flat tire while she was driving through the park.
Yesterday: A woman tripped and fell while she was getting off the bus.
Today: A man tripped and fell while he was getting on the bus.
Yesterday: A dog bit a mail carrier while he was delivering the mail.
Today: A dog bit a police officer while she was directing traffic.
Yesterday: A can of paint fell on a woman while she was walking under a ladder.
Today: Flowers fell on a man while he was walking into the clinic.
Yesterday: Someone stole a man's car while he was shopping at the mall.
Today: Someone stole a woman's bicycle while she was reading in the library.

The Activity

Students place pictures on a grid and then turn them over based on sentences they hear.

Getting Ready

Students will do this activity as a class. Make a copy of Activity Master 2 *(Listening Grid)* and Activity Master 77 *(Injury Cards)* for each student. Cut each copy of Activity Master 77 into separate cards.

❑ **1.** Give each student a *Listening Grid* and a set of *Injury Cards*.

❑ **2.** Tell students to choose nine of the cards and to place them on their grid, face up, in any order they wish.

❑ **3.** Tell students that these people had a very bad day yesterday. They all injured themselves. Say the following sentences in random order and tell students to turn over any card that you have described.

He cut himself while he was slicing bread.
She cut herself while she was slicing bread.
They cut themselves while they were slicing bread.
He cut himself while he was slicing carrots.
She cut herself while she was slicing carrots.
They cut themselves while they were slicing carrots.
He hurt himself while he was rollerblading.
She hurt herself while she was rollerblading.
They hurt themselves while they were rollerblading.
He hurt himself while he was playing tennis.
She hurt herself while she was playing tennis.
They hurt themselves while they were playing tennis.
He burned himself while he was cooking on the barbecue.
She burned herself while she was cooking on the barbecue.
They burned themselves while they were cooking on the barbecue.
He burned himself while he was baking cookies.
She burned herself while she was baking cookies.
They burned themselves while they were baking cookies.
He poked himself in the eye while he was putting on his glasses.
She poked herself in the eye while she was putting on her glasses.
They poked themselves in the eye while they were putting on their glasses.
He poked himself in the eye while he was taking out his contact lens.
She poked herself in the eye while she was taking out her contact lens.
They poked themselves in the eye while they were taking out their contact lenses.

❑ **4.** The first person to have three turned-over cards in a straight line—either vertically, horizontally, or diagonally—wins the game. Have the winner call out the sentences to check accuracy.

 **9.6** **Guess What Happened to Me!**
PANTOMIME GAME (Text page 90)

  ACTIVITY MASTER
78

The Activity

Teams compete to pantomime different mishaps.

Getting Ready

Make a copy of Activity Master 78 (*Mishap Cue Cards*) and cut it into separate cards.

❏ 1. Divide the class into two teams.

❏ 2. Write the following on the board:

_____ while _____.

❏ 3. Place the *Mishap Cue Cards* face down in a pile on a table in the front of the room.

❏ 4. Explain that each card has a *mishap* word, something bad that happened to someone, plus the word *while*. Students have to pantomime the bad thing that happened and think of a situation that was happening when that mishap occurred.

❏ 5. A student from Team 1 comes to the front of the room, picks a card, thinks of a situation (for example, *I lost my wallet while I was walking into the laundromat*), and pantomimes the event.

❏ 6. If Team 1 guesses correctly, they get to keep the card. If Team 1 doesn't guess correctly, a student from the other team must act out a situation using that card while his or her teammates attempt to guess what it is. Each team is allowed two guesses before the other team tries. If neither team guesses the mishap, the card goes back to the bottom of the pile.

The team with the most cards wins the game.

CHAPTER 10

10.1  **Guess the Situation!**
GUESSING GAME (Text page 95)

 ACTIVITY MASTER
79

The Activity

Teams compete to identify situations in which people couldn't/weren't able to do the things they wanted to do.

Getting Ready

Make a copy of Activity Master 79 *(Difficult Situation Cards)* and cut it into cards.

❏ **1.** Divide the class into four teams.

❏ **2.** Give 5 different *Difficult Situation Cards* to each team.

❏ **3.** Write the following on the board:

couldn't
weren't able to } ——————

too ——————

❏ **4.** Explain that the object of the game is for each team to create short role plays based on the situations on the cards (without saying the adjectives!). Teams take turns presenting their role plays to the class, and the other teams attempt to guess the situation using *couldn't* or *weren't able to* and *too* + adjective. If a team member raises his or her hand and guesses the situation correctly, that team gets a point. If a team guesses the situation incorrectly, another team gets a chance to guess.

The team with the most points wins the game.

10.2  **Frank & Tina: Two Unlucky People**
STORY GAME (Text page 96)

PAIRS

ACTIVITY MASTERS
80, 81,
82, 83

The Activity

Pairs of students ask each other questions to find information each of them is missing.

Getting Ready

Students will do this activity in pairs. Make copies of Activity Master 80 *(Frank's Frustrating Week! A)* and Activity Master 81 *(Tina's Terrible Week! A)* for half the class and Activity Master 82 *(Frank's Frustrating Week! B)* and Activity Master 83 *(Tina's Terrible Week! B)* for the other half of the class.

❑ **1.** Divide the class into pairs.

❑ **2.** *Give a copy of Frank's Frustrating Week! A and Tina's Terrible Week! A to one member of each pair and a copy of Frank's Frustrating Week! B and Tina's Terrible Week! B to the other.*

❑ **3.** Write the following questions on the board and have students practice saying them:

> What did Frank want to do on Monday afternoon?
> Why couldn't he go to the beach?
> Why wasn't he able to go to the beach?
>
> What did Tina want to do on Monday evening?
> Why couldn't she go to her daughter's school play?
> Why wasn't she able to go to her daughter's school play?

❑ **4.** Explain that each person has two stories with missing information. Have students use the questions on the board to discover information that is missing from their stories and then write the information in the chart. For example:

Student A: What did Frank want to do on Monday afternoon?
Student B: He wanted to go to the beach.
Student A: Why wasn't he able to go to the beach?
Student B: He had to take his son to the doctor.

❑ **5.** When students have completed the activity, have them look at their partners' paragraphs to check their answers.

The Activity

Students walk around the classroom asking each other about things they've got to do this week.

Getting Ready

Students will do this activity as a class. Make a copy of Activity Master 84 *(Things They've Got to Do)* for each student in the class.

❑ **1.** Give a copy of *Things They've Got to Do* to each student.

❑ **2.** Write the following on the board and have students practice saying it:

> A. Do you have to go to the bank this week?
> B. Yes. I've got to go to the bank.
>   No.

❑ **3.** Have students walk around the room asking each other, "Do you have to _____ this week?" When students have found someone who has got to do one of the activities on their grids, the responding student should write his or her name in that square of the grid. (Only one signature is necessary for each square.)

❑ **4.** The first student whose grid is filled with signatures is the winner of the game. Have that student then report to the class about each of the obligations. For example:

Maria has got to go to the bank.
Robert has got to buy food at the supermarket.
Alex has got to go to the doctor.

The Activity

Students play a board game that focuses on past and future ability and obligations.

Getting Ready

Students will do this activity in groups. Make a copy of Activity Master 85 *(Ability & Obligations Game)* and Activity Master 86 *(Ability Cube)* for each group. Make a cube from Activity Master 86 for each group.

Each group will need a die. You can duplicate Activity Master 22 *(Game Cube)* to make a die, or students can use a coin. Each player will also need a marker (a button or anything small).

❑ **1.** Divide the class into small groups.

❑ **2.** *Give a copy of the Ability & Obligations Game and an Ability Cube to each group. Also provide each group with a die and markers. If students use a coin as a die, the class should decide which side of the coin will indicate a move of one space and which will indicate a move of two spaces.*

❑ **3.** *Have students place their markers on Start. The group should decide who goes first. That student begins the game by rolling the cube (or flipping the coin) and moving his or her marker. If the student responds to the question or task correctly, he or she may take one more turn. (The group decides if the response is correct.) If the student doesn't respond correctly, the next student takes a turn. No one may take more than two turns at a time.*

Option 1: The first person to reach Finish is the winner.

Option 2: The game continues until each student reaches Finish. This way everybody is a winner.

 **11.1** A Complete Checkup
LISTENING GRID (Text pages 106–107)

CLASS

ACTIVITY MASTERS
2 & 87

The Activity

Students place pictures on a grid and then turn them over based on sentences they hear.

Getting Ready

Students will do this activity as a class. Make a copy of Activity Master 2 *(Listening Grid)* and Activity Master 87 *(Medical Checkup Cards)* for each student. Cut each copy of Activity Master 87 into separate cards.

❏ 1. Give each student a *Listening Grid* and a set of *Medical Checkup Cards*.

❏ 2. Tell students to choose nine of the cards and to place them on their grid, face up, in any order they wish.

❏ 3. Say the following sentences in random order and tell students to turn over any card that you have described:

> I called the clinic and made an appointment.
> I waited for the doctor.
> The nurse measured my height.
> The nurse measured my weight.
> The nurse took my blood pressure.
> The lab technician did some blood tests.
> The X-ray technician took a chest X-ray.
> The nurse led me into an examination room.
> The doctor came in, shook my hand, and said "hello."
> The doctor asked me some questions about my health.
> The doctor examined my eyes.
> The doctor examined my ears.
> The doctor examined my nose.
> The doctor examined my throat.
> The doctor listened to my heart with a stethoscope.
> The doctor took my pulse.
> The doctor did a cardiogram.
> I sat in the doctor's office and he talked with me about my health.

❏ 4. The first person to have three turned-over cards in a straight line— either vertically, horizontally, or diagonally—wins the game. Have the winner call out the sentences to check accuracy.

The Activity

Teams compete to pantomime steps in a medical checkup.

Getting Ready

Make a copy of Activity Master 87 (*Medical Checkup Cards*) and cut it into separate cards.

- ❏ **1.** Divide the class into two teams.
- ❏ **2.** Place the *Medical Checkup Cards* in a pile on a table in the front of the room.
- ❏ **3.** Two students from Team 1 come to the front of the room, pick a card, and pantomime the situation on the card.
- ❏ **4.** If Team 1 guesses the situation correctly (for example, "The nurse is taking your blood pressure"), they get to keep the card. If Team 1 doesn't guess correctly, two students from the other team must act out the situation without speaking and their teammates attempt to guess what it is. Each team is allowed two guesses before the other team tries. If neither team guesses the situation, the card goes back to the bottom of the pile.

  The team with the most cards wins the game.

The Activity

Teams compete to give appropriate, grammatically correct advice for losing weight.

Getting Ready

Make a copy of Activity Master 88 *(Count/Non-Count Cube)* and make a cube from it.

☐ **1.** Divide the class into two teams.

☐ **2.** Write the following on the board:

> If you want to lose weight, you must eat/drink _____ and _____.

☐ **3.** Explain that students will take turns rolling the cube twice and completing the sentence on the board in an appropriate and grammatically *correct* way based on the words on the cubes. For example: 1st roll of the cube: *more,* 2nd roll of the cube: *fewer.*

AN ACCEPTABLE RESPONSE
Appropriate and grammatically correct:
If you want to lose weight, you must eat more fish and fewer potatoes.

UNACCEPTABLE RESPONSES
Appropriate but not grammatically correct:
If you want to lose weight, you must eat more vegetables and fewer ice cream.

Not appropriate but grammatically correct:
If you want to lose weight, you must eat more ice cream and fewer potatoes.

Not appropriate and not grammatically correct:
If you want to lose weight, you must eat more ice cream and less potatoes.

☐ **4.** Place the *Count/Non-Count Cube* on a table in the front of the room.

☐ **5.** Have a student from Team 1 come to the front of the room, roll the cube twice, and complete the sentence on the board. If the class decides that the response is appropriate and grammatically correct, that team gets a point and Team 2 takes their turn. If the class decides that an answer is not acceptable, the team doesn't get any points for the answer and Team 2 has an opportunity to complete the statement.

The team with the most points is the winner of the game.

The Activity

Groups of students make up rules for a business, an apartment building, and a school.

Getting Ready

Students will do this activity in groups. Make a copy of Activity Master 89 *(Rules & Regulations)* for each group.

❏ **1.** Divide the class into small groups.

❏ **2.** *Give a copy of Rules & Regulations to each group. Explain that the object of the activity is for each group to create a set of rules using* must *and* mustn't *for a business, an apartment building, and a school. Have students think of a name for the business and the school and an address for the apartment building.*

❏ **3.** Allow the groups 15 minutes to complete the activity, then call on them to present their rules and regulations to the class.

❏ **4.** Have the class vote on which sets of rules for the business, the apartment building, and the school they think are the best.

The Activity

Groups give advice on things people *should* and *mustn't* do.

Getting Ready

Students will do this activity in small groups. Make a copy of Activity Master 90 *(In Our Opinion)* for each group.

❏ **1.** Divide the class into small groups.

❏ **2.** *Give each group a copy of In Our Opinion.*

❏ **3.** Have the groups agree on two things a person *should* do in each of the situations, and one thing the person *mustn't do.*

❏ **4.** Have each group designate one person to be the scribe and write the group's advice on the Activity Master.

❏ **5.** After the groups have finished their discussions, have them present their opinions to the class and react to the others' ideas.

The Activity

Students play a board game that focuses on diet, health, and giving advice.

Getting Ready

Students will do this activity in groups. Make a copy of Activity Master 91 (*Health & Advice Game*) for each group.

Each group will need a die. You can duplicate Activity Master 22 (*Game Cube*) to make a die for each group, or students can use a coin. Each player will also need a marker (a button or anything small).

❑ **1.** Divide the class into small groups.

❑ **2.** Give a copy of the *Health & Advice Game* to each group. Also provide each group with a die and markers. If students use a coin as a die, the class should decide which side of the coin will indicate a move of one space and which will indicate a move of two spaces.

❑ **3.** Have students place their markers on *Start.* The group should decide who goes first. That student begins the game by rolling the cube (or flipping the coin) and moving his or her marker. If the student responds to the question or task correctly, he or she may take one more turn. (The group decides if the response is correct.) If the student doesn't respond correctly, the next student takes a turn. No one may take more than two turns at a time.

Option 1: The first person to reach *Finish* is the winner.

Option 2: The game continues until each student reaches *Finish.* This way everybody is a winner.

12.1 **What Will You Be Doing?**
CLASSROOM SEARCH (Text page 116)

CLASS

ACTIVITY MASTER
92

The Activity

Students walk around the classroom asking each other what they will be doing this evening.

Getting Ready

Students will do this activity as a class. Make a copy of Activity Master 92 *(What Will You Be Doing?)* for each student in the class.

❑ 1. Give a copy of *What Will You Be Doing?* to each student.

❑ 2. Write the following on the board and have students practice saying it:

> *What will you be doing this evening at 8 o'clock?*

❑ 3. Have students walk around asking each other the question on the board. When students have found someone who will be doing an activity on their grids, the responding student should write his or her name in that square of the grid. (Only one signature is necessary for each square.)

❑ 4. The first student whose grid is filled with signatures is the winner of the game. Have that student then report to the class about each of the activities. For example:

> David will be reading.
> Maria will be exercising.
> Diane will be paying bills.

The Activity

Students work together to determine what Betty will be doing this week.

Getting Ready

Students will do this activity in pairs. Make copies of Activity Master 93 (*Betty's Busy Week A*) for half the class and Activity Master 94 (*Betty's Busy Week B*) for the other half of the class.

❑ **1.** Divide the class into pairs.

❑ **2.** Give a copy of *Betty's Busy Week A* to one member of each pair and a copy of *Betty's Busy Week B* to the other.

❑ **3.** Write the following conversation on the board and have students practice it:

> A. Will Betty be busy on Monday morning?
> B. Yes, she will. She'll be meeting with a client.

❑ **4.** Tell the class that each person has different information about Betty's schedule. The object of the activity is for each member of the pair to use the model on the board to find out the missing information about what Betty will be doing each day and write it in their copy of her schedule.

❑ **5.** When the pairs have completed the activity, have them tell the information that was missing from their schedule. For example:

> Student B: She'll be meeting with a client on Monday morning.
> Student A: She'll be preparing a report on Monday afternoon.

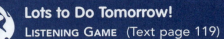
The Activity

Students ask and answer questions in order to match what they will be doing each part of the day tomorrow.

Getting Ready

Make a copy of Activity Master 95 *(Tomorrow's Plans)* and Activity Master 96 *(Tomorrow Action Cards)* for each student. Cut each Activity Master 96 into separate cards.

☐ **1.** Divide the class into pairs.

☐ **2.** Give each student a copy of *Tomorrow's Plans* and a set of *Tomorrow Action Cards.*

☐ **3.** Write the following on the board and have students practice it:

> A. Will you be reading tomorrow morning?
> B. Yes, I will.
>   No, I won't.

☐ **4.** Student A decides what he or she will be doing each part of the day tomorrow and places two or more action cards accordingly in each part of his or her schedule.

☐ **5.** Student B must arrange the activities so that they match Student A's version by asking Yes/No questions about what Student A will be doing *tomorrow morning, tomorrow afternoon, tomorrow evening,* and *tomorrow night.*

☐ **6.** When students have completed the activity, have them compare to make sure their activity cards are in the same parts of the day.

☐ **7.** Have students reverse roles and play again.

Future Continuous Game
BOARD GAME (Text page 123)

GROUPS

ACTIVITY MASTERS
22, 97, 98

The Activity

Students play a board game that focuses on the future continuous tense.

Getting Ready

Students will do this activity in groups. Make a copy of Activity Master 97 *(Future Continuous Game)* and Activity Master 98 *(Key Word Cards)* for each group. Cut each copy of Activity Master 98 into separate cards.

Each group will need a die. You can duplicate Activity Master 22 *(Game Cube)* to make a die for each group, or students can use a coin. Each player will also need a marker (a button or anything small).

❑   1. Divide the class into small groups.

❑   2. *Give a copy of the Future Continuous Game and a set of Key Word Cards to each group. Also provide each group with a die and markers. If students use a coin as a die, the class should decide which side of the coin will indicate a move of one space and which will indicate a move of two spaces.*

❑   3. Have students place their markers on *Start*. The group should decide who goes first. That student begins the game by rolling the cube (or flipping the coin) and moving his or her marker. If the student responds to the question or task correctly, he or she may take one more turn. (The group decides if the response is correct.) If the student doesn't respond correctly, the next student takes a turn. No one may take more than two turns at a time.

Option 1: The first person to reach *Finish* is the winner.

Option 2: The game continues until each student reaches *Finish*. This way everybody is a winner.

CHAPTER 13

13.1 What Are the Differences?
MEMORY GAME (Text page 127)

PAIRS

ACTIVITY MASTERS
99 & 100

The Activity
Students look at pairs of pictures and try to remember the differences between them.

Getting Ready
Students will do this activity in pairs. Make copies of Activity Master 99 *(What Are the Differences?)* and Activity Master 100 *(Complete the Conversations)* for each pair.

❑ **1.** Divide the class into pairs.

❑ **2.** Give each pair a copy of *What Are the Differences?*

❑ **3.** Tell students that they will have 3 minutes to study the pictures carefully and try to remember the differences. After they have studied the pictures, tell them to put the Activity Master aside.

❑ **4.** Next give each pair a copy of *Complete the Conversations.* Have them work together to complete them based on their memory of the pictures on Activity Master 99. In their answers, students should use the appropriate subject, object, possessive, and reflexive pronouns depending upon the situation. (Point out Example 1 on the Activity Master.)

❑ **5.** When students have completed answering the questions, have them look at Activity Master 99 again to check their answers.

Answer Key

1. He lost his in the park, and she lost hers at the beach.
2. I lost mine on the bus, and they lost theirs on the train.
3. I call her on Sunday, and she calls me on Wednesday.
4. We call him on Tuesday, and he calls us on Saturday.
5. I visit them in the winter, and they visit me in the summer.
6. We visit her in the spring, and she visits us in the fall.
7. He cut himself while he was slicing carrots, and she cut herself while she was opening a package.
8. I spilled coffee all over myself, and they spilled milk all over themselves.
9. You poked yourself in the eye, and she got wet paint all over herself.
10. You burned yourselves, and they cut themselves.

The Activity

Groups arrange a set of pictures in any order they wish and write a story about it.

Getting Ready

Students will do this activity in groups. Make a copy of Activity Master 101 *(Bob Story Cards)* for each group. Cut each Activity Master into separate cards. Also, each group will need to have some paper.

❑ **1.** Divide the class into small groups.

❑ **2.** Give each group a set of *Bob Story Cards.*

❑ **3.** Have each group lay out the pictures and decide what order to put them in. When they have decided on the order they want, have them work together to write a story about what happened to Bob last night based on the pictures.

❑ **4.** When everyone has finished, have the groups take turns telling their story to the rest of the class.

The Activity

Teams compete to answer questions with *some-* and *any-* words.

Getting Ready

Make a copy of Activity Master 102 *(Some & Any Questions 1)* and Activity Master 103 *(Some & Any Questions 2)*. Cut the Activity Masters into separate cards. You will also need a watch with a second hand or a timer for this activity.

❑ 1. Divide the class into two teams.

❑ 2. Place *Some & Any Questions 1* in a pile face-down for Team 1 to use and *Some & Any Questions 2* in a pile face-down for Team 2 to use.

❑ 3. Students from each team take turns picking a card from their team's pile. They must attempt to answer it in 5 seconds. If they are successful, their team earns a point. If not, a member of the other team has a chance to respond to that team's question before choosing their own card.

The team with the most points is the winner of the game.

Activity Masters

Activity Masters

1	Things I Like to Do	35	Comparisons! Comparisons!
2	Listening Grid	36	My Classmate's Opinions
3	The Mills Family Schedule	37	How Are They Different?
4	The Mills Family Activities	38	Memory Test
5	Happy Birthday! A	39	Problem Situations
6	Happy Birthday! B	40	Superlative Game
7	Go Shopping! Cards	41	Superlative Question Cards
8	My Kitchen	42	Superlative Sentence Cards
9	Food Cards	43	Superlative Cube
10	Kitchen A	44	Ray Roberts & His Family A
11	Kitchen B	45	Roy Roberts & His Family A
12	The Foods at Amy's Party	46	Ray Roberts & His Family B
13	A Little & A Few Match Cards	47	Roy Roberts & His Family B
14	Go Shopping! Cards	48	Adjective List
15	Shopping List A	49	Commercial Cards
16	Shopping List B	50	Main Street Directions
17	The Foods in Kevin's Kitchen	51	Main Street Maps
18	Sam's Supermarket A	52	Downtown Map A
19	Sam's Supermarket B	53	Downtown Map B
20	A Wonderful Dinner A	54	Centerville Map
21	A Wonderful Dinner B	55	Mystery Places
22	Game Cube	56	Direction Cards
23	The Food Game	57	Transportation Cards
24	Magical Mystery Cards	58	Transportation Maps
25	Questions About My Future	59	Getting Around Town Game
26	Frieda, the Fortune Teller	60	Places Around Town Cards
27	Debbie's Schedule A	61	The Best Secretary
28	Debbie's Schedule B	62	Doing Things Differently
29	Decisions! Decisions!	63	Do You Remember?
30	George, the Pessimist! A	64	Rate Yourself!
31	George, the Pessimist! B	65	Everybody Complains About Howard A
32	Think of Something!/Think of Someone!	66	Everybody Complains About Howard B
33	Let's Compare! Game	67	What Will Happen?/What Might Happen?
34	Comparison Cube		

68	Adverb & Conditional Game	86	Ability Cube
69	Consequence Cards	87	Medical Checkup Cards
70	Action Cards	88	Count/Non-Count Cube
71	What Were You Doing?	89	Rules & Regulations
72	They Were Doing Different Things	90	In Our Opinion
73	If I Remember Correctly	91	Health & Advice Game
74	Yesterday Match Cards	92	What Will You Be Doing?
75	What Happened to These People?	93	Betty's Busy Week A
76	18 Unfortunate Things!	94	Betty's Busy Week B
77	Injury Cards	95	Tomorrow's Plans
78	Mishap Cue Cards	96	Tomorrow Action Cards
79	Difficult Situation Cards	97	Future Continuous Game
80	Frank's Frustrating Week! A	98	Key Word Cards
81	Tina's Terrible Week! A	99	What Are the Differences?
82	Frank's Frustrating Week! B	100	Complete the Conversations
83	Tina's Terrible Week! B	101	Bob Story Cards
84	Things They've Got to Do	102	Some & Any Questions 1
85	Ability & Obligations Game	103	Some & Any Questions 2

- Ask other students what they like to do on the weekend.
- When you find someone who likes to do an activity on your grid, have that person write his or her name in that square.
- The first student with the most signatures wins the game.

Watch TV? Name: _____	**Go to the Movies?** Name: _____	**Write Letters?** Name: _____
Cook? Name: _____	**Go to the Beach?** Name: _____	**Read?** Name: _____
Go to the Mall? Name: _____	**Listen to Music?** Name: _____	**Plant Flowers?** Name: _____
Play Tennis? Name: _____	**Play Cards?** Name: _____	**Visit Friends?** Name: _____
Go Hiking? Name: _____	**Eat at a Restaurant?** Name: _____	**Go Dancing?** Name: _____

What did Mr. and Mrs. Mills and their six sons do yesterday, and what are they going to do tomorrow? Ask your partner questions in order to find out the answers.

- Work with a partner. (Don't show your schedule to your partner.)
- One of you arranges the Mills Family Activities cards any way he or she wishes.
- The other person asks Yes/No questions in order to match the same arrangement on his or her schedule.
- When the activity is complete, compare schedules with your partner.

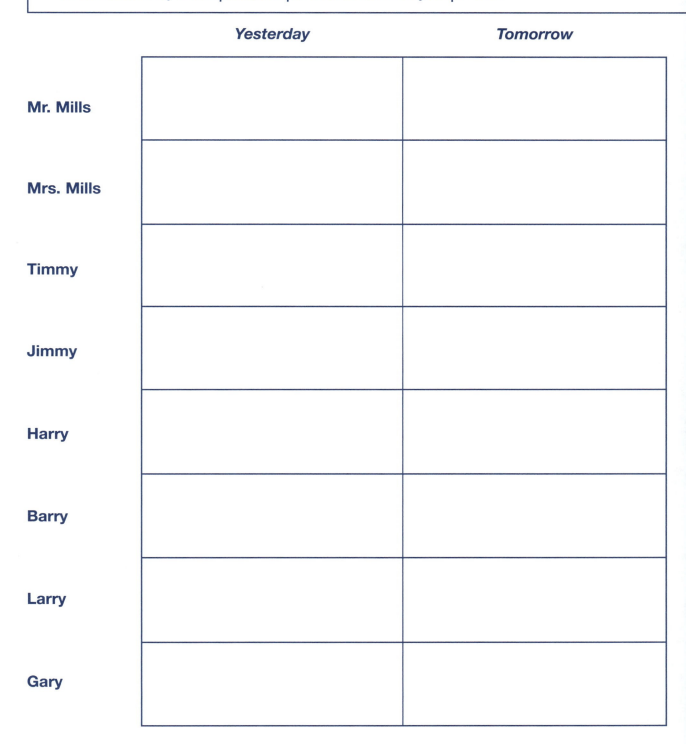

	Yesterday	Tomorrow
Mr. Mills		
Mrs. Mills		
Timmy		
Jimmy		
Harry		
Barry		
Larry		
Gary		

cook breakfast	cook dinner
drive downtown	drive to the mountains
plant flowers	plant vegetables
make pancakes	make cookies
go to the mall	go to the beach
write letters	write postcards
watch videos	watch the news
wash the dishes	wash the car

- Work with a partner. Don't look at your partner's paragraph.
- Your partner has information that you don't have, and you have information that your partner doesn't have.
- Ask questions about the missing information in your paragraph.
- Write the answers below. Then look at your partner's paragraph to check.

The Lane Family

The Lane family likes to give presents to each other. **(1)** Last year Mr. Lane gave his wife _____ for her birthday **(2)** because _____. **(3)** This year he's going to give her earrings. **(4)** Last year Mrs. Lane gave her husband a briefcase for his birthday. **(5)** This year she's going to give him _____ **(6)** because _____. The Lanes have two children—a son, Peter, and a daughter, Jenny. **(7)** Last year the Lanes gave their son, Peter, _____ for his birthday. **(8)** This year they're going to give him a sweater **(9)** because he's always cold. **(10)** Last year the Lanes gave their daughter, Jenny, perfume for her birthday. **(11)** This year they're going to give her _____ **(12)** because _____. **(13)** Last year Peter and Jenny gave their parents _____ for their anniversary. **(14)** This year they're going to give their parents a computer **(15)** because their old one doesn't work very well. Every birthday and anniversary is always a nice occasion for the Lane family.

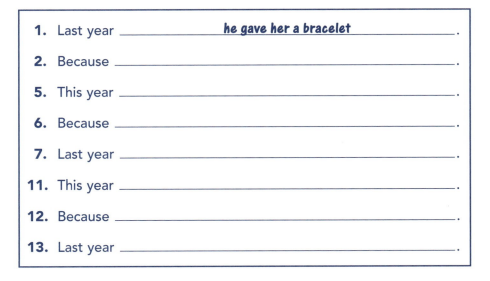

1. Last year _____ *he gave her a bracelet* _____.
2. Because _____.
5. This year _____.
6. Because _____.
7. Last year _____.
11. This year _____.
12. Because _____.
13. Last year _____.

- Work with a partner. Don't look at your partner's paragraph.
- Your partner has information that you don't have, and you have information that your partner doesn't have.
- Ask questions about the missing information in your paragraph.
- Write the answers below. Then look at your partner's paragraph to check.

The Lane Family

The Lane family likes to give presents to each other. **(1)** Last year Mr. Lane gave his wife a bracelet for her birthday **(2)** because she likes jewelry. **(3)** This year he's going to give her _____. **(4)** Last year Mrs. Lane gave her husband _____ for his birthday. **(5)** This year she's going to give him some ties **(6)** because she doesn't like his old ones. The Lanes have two children—a son, Peter, and a daughter, Jenny. **(7)** Last year the Lanes gave their son, Peter, a bicycle for his birthday. **(8)** This year they're going to give him _____ **(9)** because _____. **(10)** Last year the Lanes gave their daughter, Jenny, _____ for her birthday. **(11)** This year they're going to give her a CD player **(12)** because she likes to listen to music. **(13)** Last year Peter and Jenny gave their parents a painting for their anniversary. **(14)** This year they're going to give their parents _____ **(15)** because _____. Every birthday and anniversary is always a nice occasion for the Lane family.

3. This year _____.

4. Last year _____.

8. This year _____.

9. Because _____.

10. Last year _____.

14. This year _____.

15. Because _____.

- Work with a partner. (Don't show this kitchen to your partner.) You also each have a set of *Food Cards*.
- One of you chooses eight *Food Cards* and places two in the cabinet, two on the counter, two in the freezer, and two in the refrigerator of the kitchen below.
- The other person asks Yes/No questions in order to find out what foods are in each place and then arranges the cards in his or her kitchen based on the answers. Here is a list of foods you can ask about:

apples	chicken	ice cream	mustard	rice
bananas	coffee	ketchup	onions	salt
bread	cookies	lemons	orange juice	soda
butter	eggs	lettuce	oranges	sugar
cake	fish	mayonnaise	pears	tea
carrots	flour	meat	pepper	tomatoes
cheese	grapes	milk	potatoes	yogurt

- Compare with your partner's kitchen to see if your foods are in the same places.

2.2 The Foods in My Kitchen
LISTENING GAME
Side by Side Communication Games & Activity Masters 2, Page 6

- Work with a partner. (Don't show this kitchen to your partner.)
- Ask whether your partner has the following foods in his or her kitchen, and ask where they are:

apples	cheese	grapes	meat	pepper	tea
bananas	chicken	ice cream	milk	potatoes	tomatoes
bread	coffee	ketchup	mustard	rice	yogurt
butter	cookies	lemons	onions	salt	
cake	fish	lettuce	orange juice	soda	
carrots	flour	mayonnaise	oranges	soy sauce	

- Find two foods that are in Kitchen A, but not in Kitchen B. Also find two foods that are in Kitchen B, but not in Kitchen A. Then find two foods that are in both kitchens, but are in different places. Write the answers below.

These foods aren't in Kitchen B: _____ _____

These foods are in different places in Kitchen B: _____

_____ _____

- Work with a partner. (Don't show this kitchen to your partner.)
- Ask whether your partner has the following foods in his or her kitchen, and ask where they are:

apples	cheese	grapes	meat	pepper	tea
bananas	chicken	ice cream	milk	potatoes	tomatoes
bread	coffee	ketchup	mustard	rice	yogurt
butter	cookies	lemons	onions	salt	
cake	fish	lettuce	orange juice	soda	
carrots	flour	mayonnaise	oranges	soy sauce	

- Find two foods that are in Kitchen A, but not in Kitchen B. Also find two foods that are in Kitchen B, but not in Kitchen A. Then find two foods that are in both kitchens, but are in different places. Write the answers below.

These foods aren't in Kitchen A: _____ _____

These foods are in different places in Kitchen A:

_____ _____

- Study the scene below for one minute.
- Cover the scene and make a list of all the food items you remember. Can you remember all 25 of them?

Memory Test: *The Foods at Amy's Party*

_____   _____   _____   _____

_____   _____   _____   _____

_____   _____   _____   _____

_____   _____   _____   _____

_____   _____   _____   _____

_____   _____   _____

_____   _____   _____

_____   _____

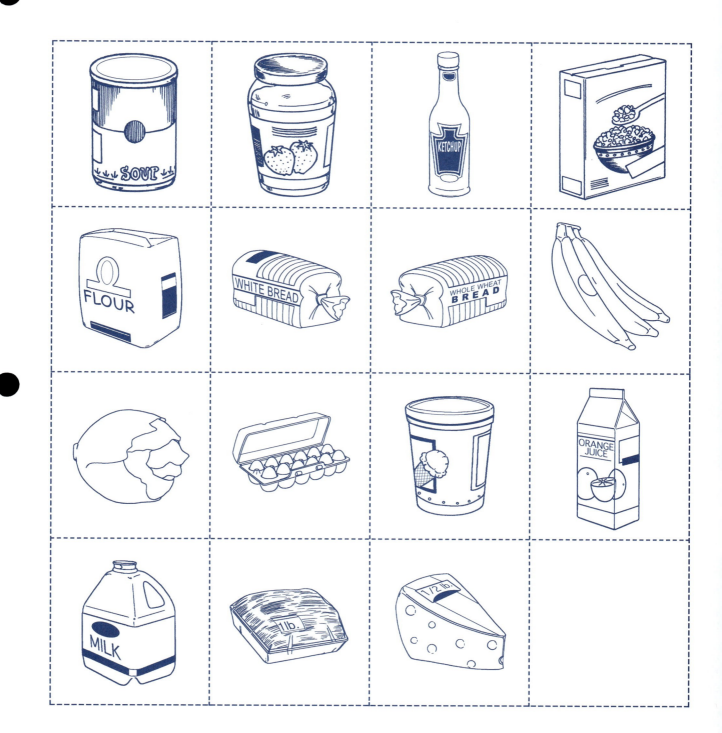

- Work with a partner. (Don't look at each other's shopping lists.)
- Ask your partner which of the following foods he or she needs at the supermarket. Also ask how much of each.

bananas	eggs	ketchup	orange juice
carrots	flour	lettuce	soup
cereal	ice cream	meat	white bread
cheese	jam	milk	whole wheat bread

- When your partner tells you what he or she needs, write the items in the list below.
- When you have identified all the foods, compare shopping lists with your partner.

My Shopping List

- ❑ one jar of jam
- ❑ two bags of flour
- ❑ one gallon of milk
- ❑ three cans of soup
- ❑ one box of cereal

- ❑ two bunches of carrots
- ❑ one dozen eggs
- ❑ two quarts of orange juice
- ❑ one loaf of whole wheat bread
- ❑ two pints of ice cream

My Partner's Shopping List

one bottle of ketchup

- Work with a partner. (Don't look at each other's shopping lists.)
- Ask your partner which of the following foods he or she needs at the supermarket. Also ask how much of each.

bananas	eggs	ketchup	orange juice
carrots	flour	lettuce	soup
cereal	ice cream	meat	white bread
cheese	jam	milk	whole wheat bread

- When your partner tells you what he or she needs, write the items in the list below.
- When you have identified all the foods, compare shopping lists with your partner.

My Shopping List

- ☐ one bottle of ketchup
- ☐ two heads of lettuce
- ☐ one bag of flour
- ☐ three pounds of cheese
- ☐ one bag of flour

- ☐ two loaves of white bread
- ☐ one bunch of bananas
- ☐ two boxes of cereal
- ☐ one pound of meat
- ☐ two dozen eggs

My Partner's Shopping List

one jar of jam

- Study the scene below for one minute.
- Cover the scene and make a list of all the food items you remember. How many can you remember?

Memory Test: *The Foods in Kevin's Kitchen*

a bottle of ketchup

- Work with a partner. (Don't show this advertisement to your partner.)
- Ask your partner questions about the prices of foods.
- Write the prices your partner tells you.
- Compare advertisements with your partner.

$am's $upermarket
This Week's Specials!

LETTUCE

ORANGES $1.29 lb.

MILK gallon

FLOUR $1.49

CHEESE 1/2 lb.

CEREAL $3.47

JAM

MAYONNAISE $1.89

KETCHUP

SOUP $1.11

WHITE BREAD

WHOLE WHEAT BREAD $2.49

ORANGE JUICE quart

- Work with a partner. (Don't show this advertisement to your partner.)
- Ask your partner questions about the prices of foods.
- Write the prices your partner tells you.
- Compare advertisements with your partner.

$am's $upermarket
This Week's Specials!

LETTUCE $1.33

ORANGES lb.

MILK $2.99 gallon

FLOUR

CHEESE $4.59 1/2 lb.

CEREAL

JAM $1.99

MAYONNAISE

KETCHUP $1.37

SOUP

WHITE BREAD $2.29

WHOLE WHEAT BREAD

ORANGE JUICE $1.87 quart

- Work with a partner. Don't look at your partner's paragraph.
- Your partner has information that you don't have, and you have information that your partner doesn't have.
- Ask questions about the missing information in your paragraph.
- Write the answers below. Then look at your partner's paragraph to check.

John, Amy, and their son, Ricky, had a wonderful dinner last night at the Riverside Restaurant. For an appetizer, John ordered **(1)** —————. He loved it. It was **(2)** —————. Amy ordered **(3)** a bowl of vegetable soup. She really enjoyed it because **(4)** it was very good. And Ricky ordered **(5)** —————. He liked it. **(6)** It was —————. For the main course, John ordered **(7)** baked fish with potatoes. He's glad he ordered it. **(8)** The fish was fantastic, and the potatoes were very tasty. Amy ordered **(9)** —————. She was very happy. **(10)** The —————, and the —————. And Ricky ordered **(11)** spaghetti and meatballs. He was also very happy. **(12)** The spaghetti was wonderful, and the meatballs were magnificent. For dessert, John ordered **(13)** —————. He loved it. **(14)** It was —————. Amy ordered **(15)** a piece of apple pie. She also loved her dessert. **(16)** It was excellent. And Ricky ordered **(17)** —————. He was very glad. **(18)** They were —————.

---

1. For an appetizer, John ordered ———— *a bowl of chicken soup* —————.

2. It was —————————————————.

5. Ricky ordered —————————————————.

6. It was —————————————————.

9. For the main course, Amy ordered —————————————.

10. The ——————————, and ——————————.

13. For dessert, John ordered ——————————————.

14. It was —————————————————.

17. For dessert, Ricky ordered ——————————————.

18. They were —————————————————.

- Work with a partner. Don't look at your partner's paragraph.
- Your partner has information that you don't have, and you have information that your partner doesn't have.
- Ask questions about the missing information in your paragraph.
- Write the answers below. Then look at your partner's paragraph to check.

John, Amy, and their son, Ricky, had a wonderful dinner last night at the Riverside Restaurant. For an appetizer, John ordered **(1)** a bowl of chicken soup. He loved it. It was **(2)** delicious. Amy ordered **(3)** _____. She really enjoyed it because **(4)** _____. And Ricky ordered **(5)** a glass of tomato juice. He liked it. **(6)** It was very fresh. For the main course, John ordered **(7)** _____. He's glad he ordered it. **(8)** The _____, and the _____. Amy ordered **(9)** broiled chicken with rice. She was very happy. **(10)** The chicken was excellent, and the rice was very good. And Ricky ordered **(11)** _____. He was also very happy. **(12)** The _____, and the _____. For dessert, John ordered **(13)** a dish of vanilla ice cream. He loved it. **(14)** It was fantastic. Amy ordered **(15)** _____. She also loved her dessert. **(16)** It was _____. And Ricky ordered **(17)** a bowl of strawberries. He was very glad. **(18)** They were out of this world.

---

3. For an appetizer, Amy ordered _____.

4. It was _____.

7. For the main course, John ordered _____.

8. The _____, and the _____.

11. Ricky ordered _____.

12. The _____, and the _____.

15. For dessert, Amy ordered _____.

16. It was _____.

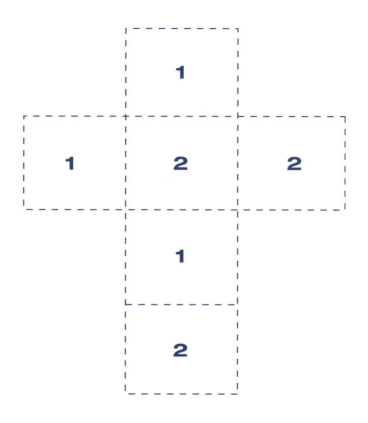

Copy and cut out this diagram to make a cube.
Fold along the lines and tape it together.

The Food Game

- Put your markers on *Start*.
- Take turns tossing the *Game Cube* (or flipping a coin) to move your marker around the board.
- Follow the instructions in each space.

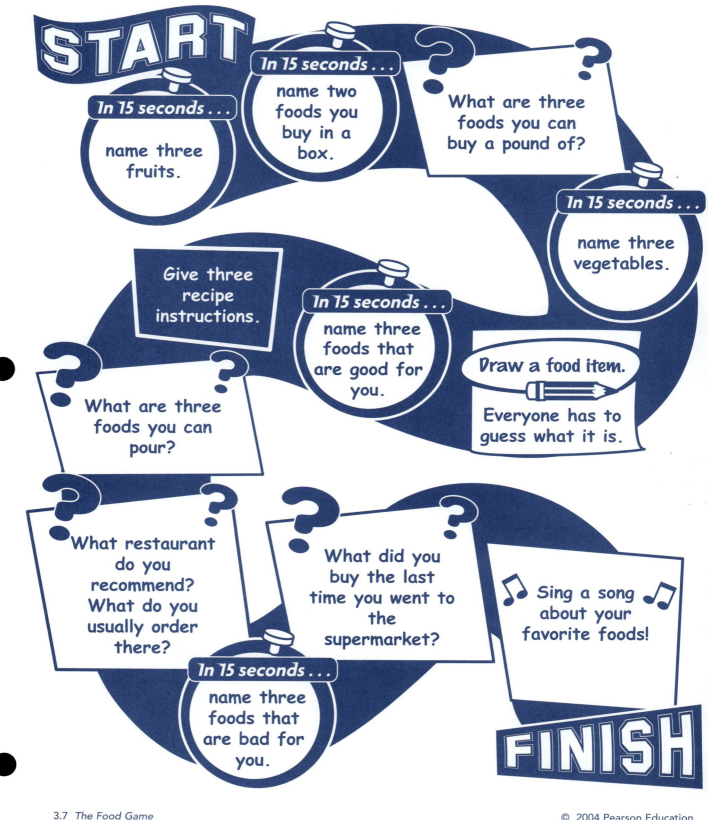

START

In 15 seconds . . . name three fruits.

In 15 seconds . . . name two foods you buy in a box.

What are three foods you can buy a pound of?

In 15 seconds . . . name three vegetables.

Give three recipe instructions.

In 15 seconds . . . name three foods that are good for you.

Draw a food item. Everyone has to guess what it is.

What are three foods you can pour?

What restaurant do you recommend? What do you usually order there?

What did you buy the last time you went to the supermarket?

In 15 seconds . . . name three foods that are bad for you.

Sing a song about your favorite foods!

FINISH

Yes!	No!	Maybe!
Probably!	Definitely!	Probably not!
Definitely not!	Yes!	Maybe!
No!	Definitely!	Probably!
Definitely not!	Maybe!	Probably not!
Definitely!	No!	Probably!
Definitely not!	Probably not!	Yes!

- Work with a partner. (Don't show these questions to your partner.)
- Complete the questions below any way you wish.
- Ask your partner the questions. Your partner is a fortune teller and knows the answers.
- When you have finished, present the questions and answers to the class.

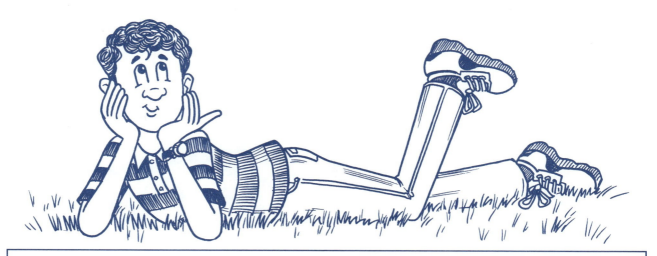

Questions About My Future

1. When will _____

_____ ?

2. How will I feel _____

_____ ?

3. Who will _____

_____ ?

4. Where will _____

_____ ?

5. How many _____

_____ ?

6. Will _____

_____ ?

- Work with a partner. (Don't show this diagram to your partner.)
- Fill in the information below any way you wish—(1) any month and year in the future, (2) an emotion, (3) a famous person, (4) a place somewhere in the world, (5) a number between one and twenty, (6) "Yes," "No," or "Maybe"
- Your partner will ask you six questions. Respond to the questions with your answers.
- When you have finished, present the questions and answers to the class.

1. a month and a year

_____

2. an emotion

_____

3. a famous person

_____

4. a place somewhere in the world

_____

5. a number between 1 and 20

_____

6. Yes, No, or Maybe

_____

Debbie can't decide what she's going to do this week.

- Work with a partner. (Don't show this schedule to your partner.)
- Ask your partner questions about what Debbie might do on different days of the week.
- Write the answers in the schedule below.
- Compare schedules with your partner.

This Week's Schedule

Monday

She might go to the beach, or she might go to the park.

Tuesday

_____

Wednesday

She might go to the movies, or she might stay home.

Thursday

_____

Friday

She might go to work, or she might take a day off.

Saturday

_____

Debbie can't decide what she's going to do this week.

- Work with a partner. (Don't show this schedule to your partner.)
- Ask your partner questions about what Debbie might do on different days of the week.
- Write the answers in the schedule below.
- Compare schedules with your partner.

This Week's Schedule

Monday

_____

Tuesday

She might go to the gym, or she might go dancing.

Wednesday

_____

Thursday

She might cook dinner, or she might go to a restaurant.

Friday

_____

Saturday

She might go shopping, or she might clean her apartment.

- Work with a partner. Your partner can't decide what he or she is going to do.
- Ask your partner questions 1 through 6 and write the answers in the chart.
- Think of four more questions to ask your partner and write your partner's answers.
- Tell the class about your partner's plans.

	I might . . .	or I might . . .
1. What are you going to have for dinner tonight?		
2. What are you going to watch on TV tonight?		
3. What are you going to wear tomorrow?		
4. What are you going to do this weekend?		
5. When are you going to clean your house or apartment?		
6. Where are you going to go for your next vacation?		
7.		
8.		
9.		
10.		

- Work with a partner. Don't look at your partner's paragraph.
- Your partner has information that you don't have, and you have information that your partner doesn't have.
- Ask questions about the missing information in your paragraph.
- Write the answers below. Then look at your partner's paragraph to check.

Everybody is upset with George. Why? Because George is a pessimist. He always thinks something bad is going to happen. George's co-workers are upset with him. **(1)** ——————— **(2)** because ———————. George's brother is upset with him. **(3)** George won't play tennis with him tomorrow afternoon **(4)** because he's afraid he might break his arm. George's sister is upset with him. **(5)** ——————— **(6)** because ———————. George's uncle is upset with him. **(7)** George won't go jogging with him on Wednesday **(8)** because he's afraid he might catch a cold. George's girlfriend is upset with him. **(9)** ——————— **(10)** because ———————. George's friends are upset with him. **(11)** He won't play basketball with them this Friday night **(12)** because he's afraid he might hurt his back. George's aunt is upset with him. **(13)** ——————— **(14)** because ———————. George's cousins are upset with him. **(15)** He won't play baseball with them on Sunday **(16)** because he's afraid he might get hit in the eye. And George's parents are upset with him. **(17)** ——————— **(18)** because ———————. You can see why everybody is upset with George!

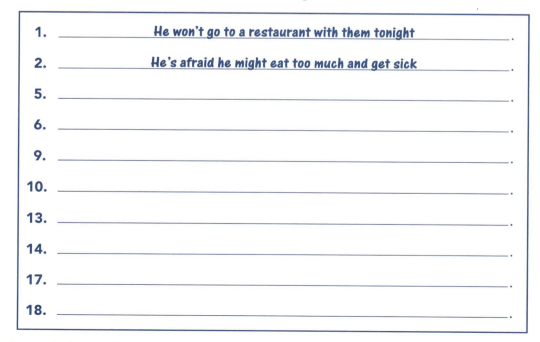

1. _He won't go to a restaurant with them tonight_ .
2. _He's afraid he might eat too much and get sick_ .
5. ————————————————————————— .
6. ————————————————————————— .
9. ————————————————————————— .
10. ———————————————————————— .
13. ———————————————————————— .
14. ———————————————————————— .
17. ———————————————————————— .
18. ———————————————————————— .

- Work with a partner. Don't look at your partner's paragraph.
- Your partner has information that you don't have, and you have information that your partner doesn't have.
- Ask questions about the missing information in your paragraph.
- Write the answers below. Then look at your partner's paragraph to check.

Everybody is upset with George. Why? Because George is a pessimist. He always thinks something bad is going to happen. George's co-workers are upset with him. **(1)** He won't go to a restaurant with them tonight **(2)** because he's afraid he might eat too much and get sick. George's brother is upset with him. **(3)** _____ **(4)** because _____. George's sister is upset with him. **(5)** He won't see a play with her tomorrow night **(6)** because he's afraid he might fall asleep. George's uncle is upset with him. **(7)** _____ **(8)** because _____. George's girlfriend is upset with him. **(9)** He won't go dancing with her on Thursday **(10)** because he's afraid he might step on her feet. George's friends are upset with him. **(11)** _____ **(12)** because _____. George's aunt is upset with him. **(13)** He won't go sailing with her this Saturday afternoon **(14)** because he's afraid he might get seasick. George's cousins are upset with him. **(15)** _____ **(16)** because _____. And George's parents are upset with him. **(17)** He won't go to their party this Sunday night **(18)** because he's afraid he might have a terrible time. You can see why everybody is upset with George!

3. _____.

4. _____.

7. _____.

8. _____.

11. _____.

12. _____.

15. _____.

16. _____.

- Work with a partner.
- Write your answers in the charts below.
- Report your comparisons to the class.

Think of something that's . . .

1. large: _____

2. small: _____

3. fast: _____

4. soft: _____

5. fancy: _____

6. quiet: _____

7. light: _____

8. delicious: _____

9. comfortable: _____

10. beautiful: _____

11. powerful: _____

Think of something that's . . .

larger: _____

smaller: _____

faster: _____

softer: _____

fancier: _____

quieter: _____

lighter: _____

more delicious: _____

more comfortable: _____

more beautiful: _____

more powerful: _____

Think of a famous person who is . . .

1. pretty: _____

2. nice: _____

3. friendly: _____

4. handsome: _____

5. interesting: _____

6. intelligent: _____

7. talented: _____

Think of a famous person who is . . .

prettier: _____

nicer: _____

friendlier: _____

more handsome: _____

more interesting: _____

more intelligent: _____

more talented: _____

Let's Compare! Game

- Put your markers on *Start.*
- Take turns tossing the Game Cube (or flipping a coin) to move your marker around the board.
- Roll the Comparison Cube and make a comparative statement with *–er* or *more.*

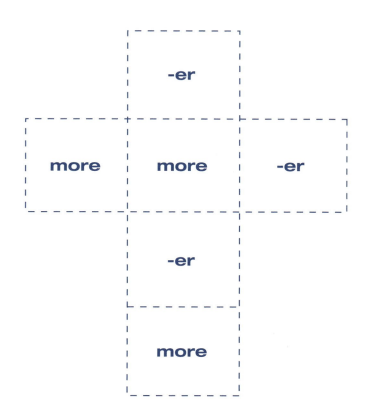

- Work with a partner to decide which of the choices below you prefer.
- Tell your preferences by making 3 comparisons using any of the following adjectives.
- Report your comparisons to the class.

attractive	cold	exciting	healthy	powerful	safe
beautiful	comfortable	expensive	hot	pretty	small
busy	convenient	fast	intelligent	quiet	ugly
cheap	delicious	friendly	large	reliable	useful

1.

a sedan? a sports car?

_____

_____

_____

2.

a house? a condominium?

_____

_____

_____

3.

French food? fast food?

_____

_____

_____

4.

a dog? a cat?

_____

_____

_____

5.

a notebook computer? a desktop computer?

_____

_____

_____

6.

a vacation in Tahiti? a vacation in London?

_____

_____

_____

5.3 *Which Do You Prefer?*
PAIR DISCUSSION
Side by Side Communication Games & Activity Masters 2, Page 24

- Interview a classmate.
- Write your classmate's answers in the questionnaire.
- Report your classmate's responses to the class.

My Classmate: _____

1. Which is more convenient—the newspaper or the Internet?	
2. Which is more difficult—English or math?	
3. Which is cuter—a dog or a cat?	
4. Which is more delicious—vanilla ice cream or chocolate ice cream?	
5. Which is more useful—a desktop computer or a laptop computer?	
6. Which is more exciting—a science fiction movie or an adventure movie?	
7. Which is more beautiful—the piano or the violin?	
8. Which is more important——love or money?	
9.	
10.	
11.	
12.	

- Spend 3 minutes looking very carefully at each of the following pairs of pictures.
- Put the Activity Master away and see how many of these differences you can remember.

Jane's office   John's office   your computer   the Jones's computer

Rick's dog   Rita's dog   your family's new chair   your neighbors' new chair

Walter's car   his parents' car   your family's garden   your Aunt Martha's garden

the Wilsons' cat   your cat   Jack's meatloaf   Jack's mother's meatloaf

our TV   the Taylors' TV   Valerie's grades   her brother's grades

your apartment   your neighbors' apartment   Donna's parrot   Donald's parrot

- Answer the questions below using *mine, his, hers, ours, theirs* in your answers.
- Look at Activity Master 37 again to check your answers. How many did you remember?

1. What's the difference between Jane's office and John's office?

   clean: _____ Hers is cleaner than his. _____

2. What's the difference between your computer and the Jones's computer?

   powerful: _____

3. What's the difference between Rick's dog and Rita's dog?

   friendly: _____

4. What's the difference between your family's new chair and your neighbors' new chair?

   comfortable: _____

5. What's the difference between Walter's car and his parents' car?

   old: _____

6. What's the difference between your family's garden and your Aunt Martha's garden?

   pretty: _____

7. What's the difference between the Wilsons' cat and your cat?

   cute: _____

8. What's the difference between Jack's meatloaf and his mother's meatloaf?

   delicious: _____

9. What's the difference between our TV and the Taylors' TV?

   big: _____

10. What's the difference between Valerie's grades and her brother's grades?

    good: _____

11. What's the difference between your apartment and your neighbors' apartment?

    warm: _____

12. What's the difference between Donna's parrot and Donald's parrot?

    talkative: _____

- Work in groups of three.
- Student A picks one of the following cards and reads the situation.
- Student B gives advice, then Student C reacts to the advice.
- The group should then discuss each situation and decide on the best advice.
- For the next problem, Student B picks the card, Student C gives advice, and Student A reacts. Continue switching roles until all the problem situations have been discussed.
- Report the group's conclusions to the class.

I'm going to a very fancy party. What should I wear?	It's late at night and Richard can't sleep. What should he do?
Mrs. Williams wants to buy a special birthday present for her husband. What should she buy him?	Timothy wants to go out with Melanie, but he's very shy. He's afraid to ask her out. What should he do?
Mr. and Mrs. Blake are upset. Their teenage son doesn't like to do his homework. Every day he comes home from school and watches TV. What should they do?	George is always late. He's late for appointments. He sometimes doesn't get up on time and he's late for work. George's wife is very upset with him. What should she do?
Robert and his girlfriend want to go out for a special dinner. Where should they go?	Michael has very loud neighbors. They make noise all the time. What should he do about it?
I have a very bad stomachache. What should I do?	A thief stole my bicycle! What should I do?
Rita is at work. She has a lot of important things to do, but she has a terrible headache. What should she do?	Helen is very upset. The streets in her city aren't as clean as they used to be. What should she do?

5.6 *Good Advice*
GROUP DISCUSSION
Side by Side Communication Games & Activity Masters 2, Page 27

- Put your markers on *Start.*
- Take turns tossing the Game Cube (or flipping a coin) to move your marker around the board.
- Follow the instructions in each square.

Pick a Superlative Question Card ANSWER THE QUESTION.

Point to three big things in your classroom. Tell which is the BIGGEST!

Roll the Superlative Cube IS IT -est OR *most?* TELL ABOUT SOMEONE IN YOUR FAMILY.

START

Pick a Superlative Question Card ANSWER THE QUESTION.

FINISH

Superlative Question Cards

Pick a Superlative Sentence Card COMPLETE THE SENTENCE.

Roll the Superlative Cube IS IT -est OR *most?* SING ABOUT YOURSELF!

Superlative Sentence Cards

Roll the Superlative Cube IS IT -est OR *most?* TELL ABOUT SOMEONE IN YOUR ENGLISH CLASS.

Pick a Superlative Sentence Card COMPLETE THE SENTENCE.

Pick a Superlative Question Card ANSWER THE QUESTION.

Roll the Superlative Cube IS IT -est OR *most?* TELL ABOUT SOMETHING IN YOUR CITY OR TOWN.

Look around your classroom. What is the smallest thing you see? Draw it! Everyone has to guess.

Roll the Superlative Cube IS IT -est OR *most?* TELL ABOUT A FAMOUS PERSON.

6.1 *Superlative Game*
BOARD GAME
Side by Side Communication Games & Activity Masters 2, Page 28

Who is the most interesting person you know? Tell why.

What is the oldest building in your city or town?

What is the tallest building in your city or town?

In your opinion, who is the most talented movie star?

Which restaurant in your city or town has the most delicious food?

Who is the busiest person in your family? Tell why.

What is the longest English word you know?

What is the saddest song you know? Tell why.

In your opinion, what is the easiest subject in school? Tell why.

In your opinion, what is the most difficult subject in school? Tell why.

In your opinion, who is the most important person in your country? Tell why.

What are the healthiest foods you can buy at the supermarket?

In your opinion, what is the most boring subject in school? Tell why.

Who is the funniest person you know? Tell why.

Who is the most outgoing person you know?

Who is the most athletic person you know? Tell why.

In your opinion, what is the most beautiful language?

In your opinion, who is the most important person in the world? Tell why.

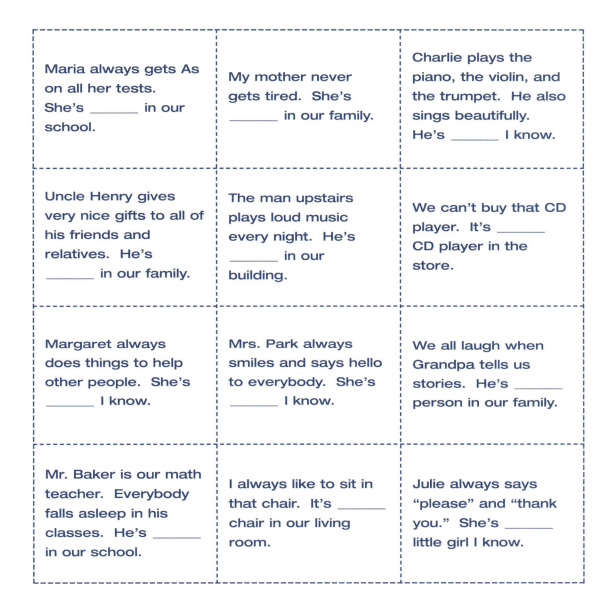

Maria always gets As on all her tests. She's _____ in our school.

My mother never gets tired. She's _____ in our family.

Charlie plays the piano, the violin, and the trumpet. He also sings beautifully. He's _____ I know.

Uncle Henry gives very nice gifts to all of his friends and relatives. He's _____ in our family.

The man upstairs plays loud music every night. He's _____ in our building.

We can't buy that CD player. It's _____ CD player in the store.

Margaret always does things to help other people. She's _____ I know.

Mrs. Park always smiles and says hello to everybody. She's _____ I know.

We all laugh when Grandpa tells us stories. He's _____ person in our family.

Mr. Baker is our math teacher. Everybody falls asleep in his classes. He's _____ in our school.

I always like to sit in that chair. It's _____ chair in our living room.

Julie always says "please" and "thank you." She's _____ little girl I know.

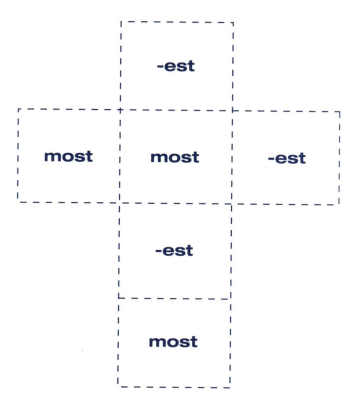

- Work with a partner. Don't look at your partner's paragraph.
- Your partner has information that you don't have, and you have information that your partner doesn't have.
- Ask questions about the missing information in your paragraph.
- Write the answers below. Then look at your partner's paragraph to check.

Ray Roberts & His Family

(1) Ray Roberts is very _____. **(2)** In fact, everybody says he's _____ person they know. Ray's wife's name is Rachel. **(3)** Rachel is very capable. **(4)** In fact, Ray tells everybody that Rachel is the most capable person he knows. Ray and Rachel have two children—a son, Ron, and a daughter, Rita. **(5)** Ron is very _____. **(6)** In fact, everybody says he's _____ boy in town. **(7)** And Rita is very intelligent. **(8)** Everybody says that Rita is the most intelligent girl in her school. Ray also has a dog named Rover. **(9)** Rover is very _____. **(10)** In fact, people say that Rover is _____ dog on River Street. **(11)** Ray and Rachel's house is very pretty. **(12)** All the neighbors say that their house is the prettiest house in the neighborhood. **(13)** And their garage is very _____. **(14)** Everybody knows that Ray and Rachel's garage is _____ garage in town. **(15)** You can see why everybody really likes Ray Roberts and his family.

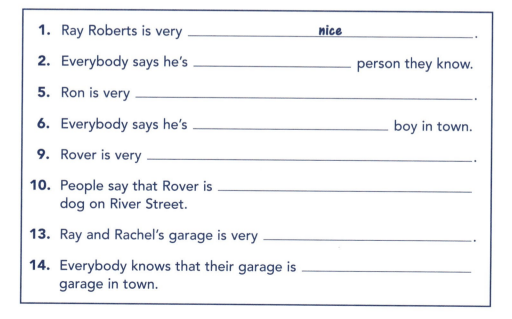

1. Ray Roberts is very _____ *nice* _____.
2. Everybody says he's _____ person they know.
5. Ron is very _____.
6. Everybody says he's _____ boy in town.
9. Rover is very _____.
10. People say that Rover is _____ dog on River Street.
13. Ray and Rachel's garage is very _____.
14. Everybody knows that their garage is _____ garage in town.

- Work with a partner. Don't look at your partner's paragraph.
- Your partner has information that you don't have, and you have information that your partner doesn't have.
- Ask questions about the missing information in your paragraph.
- Write the answers below. Then look at your partner's paragraph to check.

Roy Roberts & His Family

Roy is Ray's brother. Ray and Roy are very different. Ray is nice, but Roy isn't. **(1)** In fact, he's very mean. **(2)** Everybody says he's the meanest person they know. Roy's wife's name is Roz. **(3)** Roz is very _____. **(4)** In fact, Roy tells everybody that Roz is _____ person he knows. Roy and Roz have two children—a son, Richard, and a daughter, Rhoda. **(5)** Richard is very sloppy. **(6)** In fact, everybody says he's the sloppiest boy in town. **(7)** And Rhoda is very _____. **(8)** Everybody says that Rhoda is _____ girl in her school. Roy also has a dog named Rex. **(9)** Rex is very loud. **(10)** In fact, people say that Rex is the loudest dog on Rice Road. **(11)** Roy and Roz's house is very _____. **(12)** All the neighbors say that their house is _____ house in the neighborhood. **(13)** And their garage is very messy. **(14)** In fact, everybody knows that Roy and Roz's garage is the messiest garage in town. **(15)** You can see why _____ likes Roy Roberts and his family.

---

3. Roz is very _____.

4. Roy tells everybody that she's _____ person they know.

7. Rhoda is very _____.

8. Everybody says that she's _____ girl in her school.

11. Roy and Roz's house is very _____.

12. All the neighbors say that it's _____ house in the neighborhood.

15. _____ likes Roy Roberts and his family.

- Work with a partner. Don't look at your partner's paragraph.
- Your partner has information that you don't have, and you have information that your partner doesn't have.
- Ask questions about the missing information in your paragraph.
- Write the answers below. Then look at your partner's paragraph to check.

Ray Roberts & His Family

(1) Ray Roberts is very nice. (2) In fact, everybody says he's the nicest person they know. Ray's wife's name is Rachel. (3) Rachel is very _____. (4) In fact, Ray tells everybody that Rachel is _____ person he knows. Ray and Rachel have two children—a son, Ron, and a daughter, Rita. (5) Ron is very talented. (6) In fact, everybody says he's the most talented boy in town. (7) And Rita is very _____. (8) Everybody says that Rita is _____ girl in her school. Ray also has a dog named Rover. (9) Rover is very friendly. (10) In fact, people say that Rover is the friendliest dog on River Street. (11) Ray and Rachel's house is very _____. (12) All the neighbors say that their house is _____ house in the neighborhood. (13) And their garage is very neat. (14) Everybody knows that Ray and Rachel's garage is the neatest garage in town. (15) You can see why _____ really likes Ray Roberts and his family.

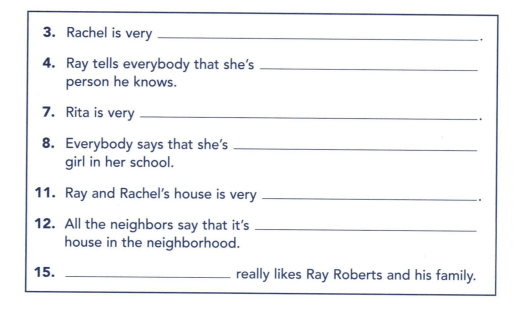

3. Rachel is very _____.

4. Ray tells everybody that she's _____ person he knows.

7. Rita is very _____.

8. Everybody says that she's _____ girl in her school.

11. Ray and Rachel's house is very _____.

12. All the neighbors say that it's _____ house in the neighborhood.

15. _____ really likes Ray Roberts and his family.

- Work with a partner. Don't look at your partner's paragraph.
- Your partner has information that you don't have, and you have information that your partner doesn't have.
- Ask questions about the missing information in your paragraph.
- Write the answers below. Then look at your partner's paragraph to check.

Roy Roberts & His Family

Roy is Ray's brother. Ray and Roy are very different. Ray is nice, but Roy isn't. **(1)** In fact, he's very _____. **(2)** Everybody says he's _____ person they know. Roy's wife's name is Roz. **(3)** Roz is very lazy. **(4)** In fact, Roy tells everybody that Roz is the laziest person he knows. Roy and Roz have two children—a son, Richard, and a daughter, Rhoda. **(5)** Richard is very _____. **(6)** In fact, everybody says he's _____ boy in town. **(7)** And Rhoda is very boring. **(8)** Everybody says that Rhoda is the most boring girl in her school. Roy also has a dog named Rex. **(9)** Rex is very _____. **(10)** In fact, people say that Rex is _____ dog on Rice Road. **(11)** Roy and Roz's house is very ugly. **(12)** All the neighbors say that their house is the ugliest house in the neighborhood. **(13)** And their garage is very _____. **(14)** In fact, everybody knows that Roy and Roz's garage is _____ garage in town. **(15)** You can see why nobody likes Roy Roberts and his family.

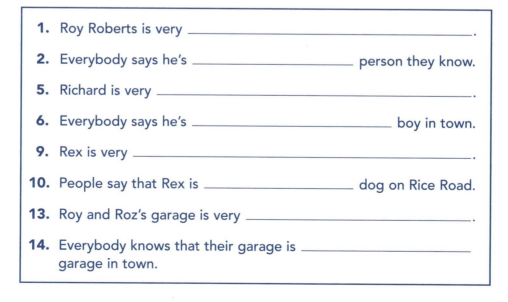

1. Roy Roberts is very _____.
2. Everybody says he's _____ person they know.
5. Richard is very _____.
6. Everybody says he's _____ boy in town.
9. Rex is very _____.
10. People say that Rex is _____ dog on Rice Road.
13. Roy and Roz's garage is very _____.
14. Everybody knows that their garage is _____ garage in town.

attractive	handsome	popular
beautiful	happy	powerful
big	healthy	pretty
bright	heavy	quiet
busy	helpful	reliable
capable	high	rich
cheap	honest	romantic
clean	hospitable	safe
comfortable	inexpensive	shiny
convenient	intelligent	short
cute	interesting	slow
delicious	kind	small
dependable	large	smart
difficult	light	soft
easy	lightweight	spicy
elegant	little	sympathetic
energetic	long	talented
enormous	loud	talkative
exciting	low	tall
expensive	magnificent	tasty
fancy	modern	tiny
fantastic	neat	uncomfortable
fashionable	new	understanding
fast	nice	useful
friendly	old	warm
funny	outgoing	wide
generous	patient	wonderful
good	polite	young

The Royal Restaurant

Brite-White Toothpaste

The ABC English School

Dave's Department Store

Ed's Electronics Store

Patty's Pet Shop

Vicky's Videos

Al's Used Cars

Peterson for President!

Visit (Your City)!

Walk up Main Street and you'll see it on the right, next to the bank.

Walk up Main Street and you'll see it on the right, next to the park.

Walk up Main Street and you'll see it on the left, next to the bank.

Walk up Main Street and you'll see it on the left, next to the park.

Walk up Main Street and you'll see it on the right, across from the bank.

Walk up Main Street and you'll see it on the right, across from the park.

Walk up Main Street and you'll see it on the left, across from the bank.

Walk up Main Street and you'll see it on the left, across from the park.

Walk up Main Street and you'll see it on the right, between the bank and the park.

Walk up Main Street and you'll see it on the left, between the bank and the park.

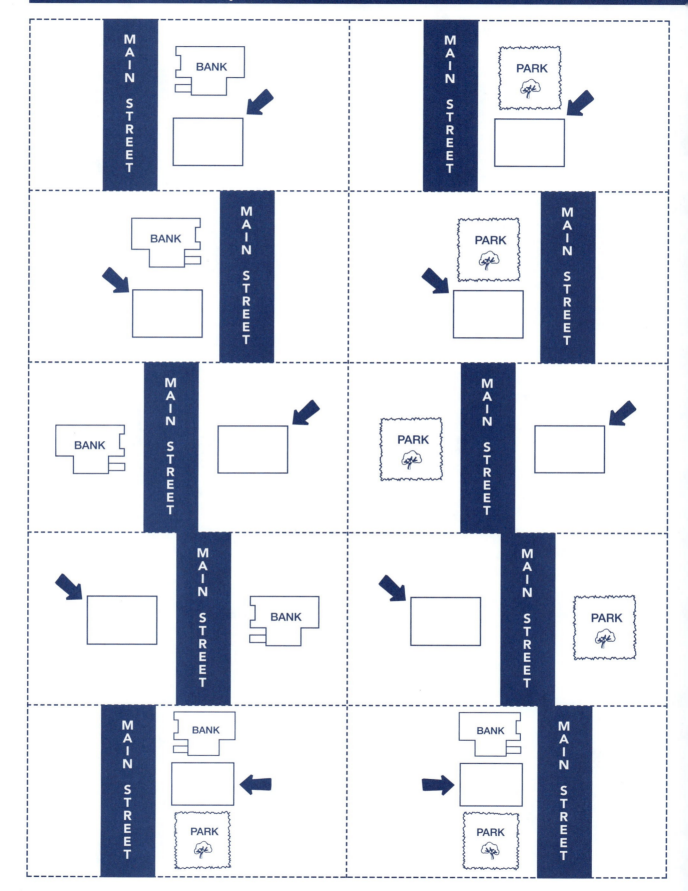

- Work with a partner. (Don't show this map to your partner.)
- Ask your partner directions to the following places:

shoe store	library	police station	hospital
park	parking lot	supermarket	

- After you get the directions, write the names on the places.
- Compare maps with your partner.

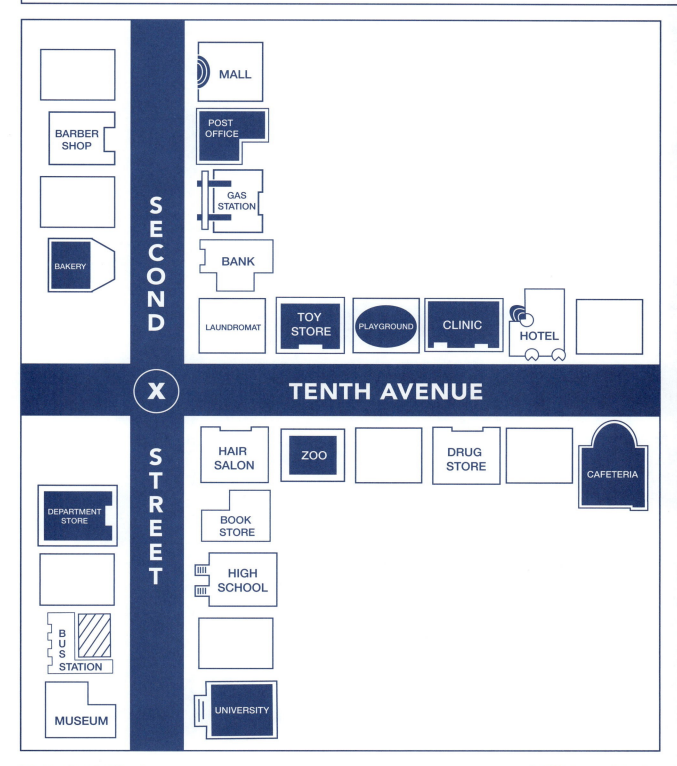

- Work with a partner. (Don't show this map to your partner.)
- Ask your partner directions to the following places:

  post office   museum   toy store

  clinic   hair salon   book store

- After you get the directions, write the names on the places.
- Compare maps with your partner.

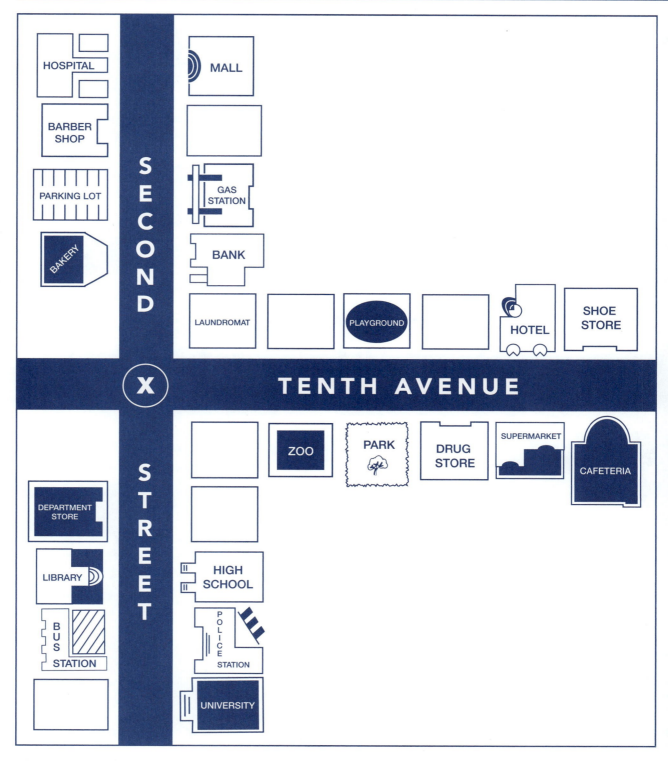

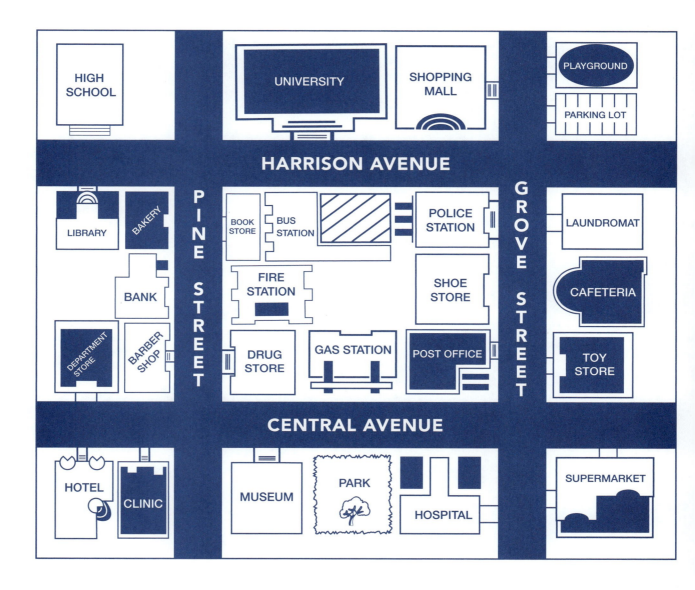

bank	barber shop	book store
bus station	cafeteria	clinic
department store	fire station	high school
hospital	hotel	library
museum	park	playground
shoe store	shopping mall	university

You're in front of the library on Harrison Avenue. Walk along Harrison Avenue to Grove Street and turn right. Walk down Grove Street and you'll see this place on the right, across from the supermarket.
[Mystery Place: hospital]

You're at the hotel on Central Avenue. Walk along Central Avenue to Pine Street and turn left. Walk up Pine Street and you'll see this place on the left, next to the barber shop. *[Mystery Place: bank]*

You're in front of the bakery on Pine Street. Walk down Pine Street to Central Avenue and turn left. Walk along Central Avenue to Grove Street and turn left again. Walk up Grove Street and you'll see this place on the left, between the post office and the police station.
[Mystery Place: shoe store]

You're in front of the fire station on Pine Street. Walk down Pine Street to Central Avenue and turn left. Walk along Central Avenue to Grove Street and turn left again. Walk up Grove Street and you'll see this place on the right, next to the toy store. *[Mystery Place: cafeteria]*

You're in front of the shoe store on Grove Street. Walk up Grove Street to Harrison Avenue and turn left. Walk along Harrison Avenue and you'll see this place on the right, across from the bus station. *[Mystery Place: university]*

You're in front of the department store on Central Avenue. Walk along Central Avenue to Pine Street and turn left. Walk up Pine Street and you'll see this place on the right, across from the bakery. *[Mystery Place: book store]*

You're in front of the fire station on Pine Street. Walk up Pine Street to Harrison Avenue and turn right. Walk along Harrison Avenue to Grove Street and turn left. Walk up Grove Street and you'll see this place on the right, next to the parking lot. *[Mystery Place: playground]*

You're on Central Avenue at the place across from the gas station. Walk along Central Avenue to Grove Street and turn left. Walk up Grove Street and you'll see this place on the left, across from the playground and the parking lot. *[Mystery Place: shopping mall]*

You're in front of the high school on Harrison Avenue. Walk along Harrison Avenue to Pine Street and turn right. Walk down Pine Street to Central Avenue and turn left. Walk along Central Avenue and you'll see this place on the right, across from the gas station. *[Mystery Place: park]*

You're in front of the shoe store on Grove Street. Walk up Grove Street to Harrison Avenue and turn left. Walk along Harrison Avenue to Pine Street and turn left again. Walk down Pine Street and you'll see this place on the right, across from the drug store. *[Mystery Place: barber shop]*

You're at the supermarket on Central Avenue. Walk along Central Avenue to Pine Street and turn right. Walk up Pine Street to Harrison Avenue and turn left. Walk along Harrison Avenue and you'll see this place on the left, across from the high school. *[Mystery Place: library]*

You're in front of the university on Harrison Avenue. Walk along Harrison Avenue to Pine Street and turn left. Walk down Pine Street to Central Avenue and turn right. Walk along Central Avenue and you'll see this place on the left, next to the clinic. *[Mystery Place: hotel]*

You're in front of the parking lot on Grove Street. Walk down Grove Street to Central Avenue and turn right. Walk along Central Avenue and you'll see this place on the left, across from the drug store. *[Mystery Place: museum]*

You're in front of the police station on Grove Street. Walk down Grove Street to Central Avenue and turn right. Walk along Central Avenue and you'll see this place on the right, across from the hotel. *[Mystery Place: department store]*

You're at the playground on Grove Street. Walk down Grove Street to Central Avenue and turn right. Walk along Central Avenue and you'll see this place on the left, next to the hotel. *[Mystery Place: clinic]*

You're at the cafeteria on Grove Street. Walk up Grove Street to Harrison Avenue and turn left. Walk along Harrison Avenue and you'll see this place on the left, across from the university. *[Mystery Place: bus station]*

You're at the park on Central Avenue. Walk along Central Avenue to Pine Street and turn right. Walk up Pine Street and you'll see this place on the right, next to the drug store. *[Mystery Place: fire station]*

You're in front of the toy store on Grove Street. Walk up Grove Street to Harrison Avenue and turn left. Walk along Harrison Avenue and you'll see this place on the right, across from the library. *[Mystery Place: high school]*

To get to the library, take the Third Avenue bus and get off at First Street. Walk up First Street and you'll see it on the right.

To get to the bakery, take the Third Avenue bus and get off at First Street. Walk up First Street and you'll see it on the left.

To get to the bank, take the First Avenue bus and get off at First Street. Walk up First Street and you'll see it on the right.

To get to the zoo, take the First Avenue bus and get off at First Street. Walk up First Street and you'll see it on the left.

To get to the hotel, take the Third Avenue bus and get off at Third Street. Walk up Third Street and you'll see it on the right.

To get to the clinic, take the Third Avenue bus and get off at Third Street. Walk up Third Street and you'll see it on the left.

To get to the hospital, take the First Avenue bus and get off at Third Street. Walk up Third Street and you'll see it on the right.

To get to the park, take the First Avenue bus and get off at Third Street. Walk up Third Street and you'll see it on the left.

To get to the pet shop, take the Fifth Avenue bus and get off at Sixth Street. Walk up Sixth Street and you'll see it on the right.

To get to the restaurant, take the Fifth Avenue bus and get off at Sixth Street. Walk up Sixth Street and you'll see it on the left.

To get to the supermarket, take the Sixth Avenue bus and get off at Sixth Street. Walk up Sixth Street and you'll see it on the right.

To get to the toy store, take the Sixth Avenue bus and get off at Sixth Street. Walk up Sixth Street and you'll see it on the left.

To get to the museum, take the Fifth Avenue bus and get off at Fifth Street. Walk up Fifth Street and you'll see it on the right.

To get to the cafeteria, take the Fifth Avenue bus and get off at Fifth Street. Walk up Fifth Street and you'll see it on the left.

To get to the church, take the Sixth Avenue bus and get off at Fifth Street. Walk up Fifth Street and you'll see it on the right.

To get to the motel, take the Sixth Avenue bus and get off at Fifth Street. Walk up Fifth Street and you'll see it on the left.

- Work with a partner. (Don't show these maps to your partner.)
- One of you reads the directions on the Transportation Cards.
- The other person listens and writes the name of each place under the correct diagram.
- Compare directions and maps with your partner.

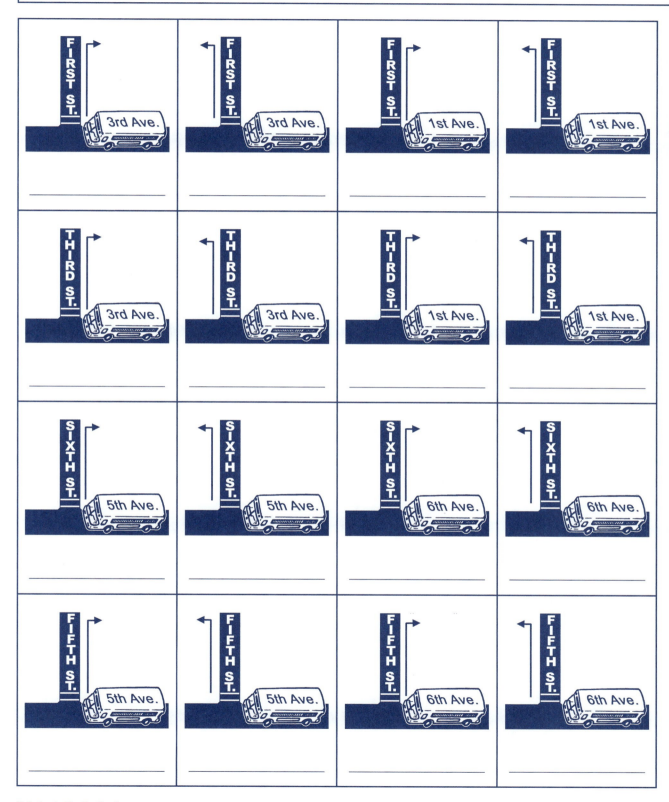

- Put your markers on *Start*.
- Take turns tossing the Game Cube (or flipping a coin) to move your marker around the board.
- Follow the instructions in each space.

START

FINISH

Ask for directions to a place in your city or town.

What are 3 places you go by bus?

Ask a classmate for directions. After you hear them, repeat them back.

What are 4 ways to say "thank you"?

Places Around Town Cards

Pick a *Places Around Town Card*
GIVE DIRECTIONS FROM YOUR SCHOOL TO THAT PLACE.

You want to go to the zoo. Ask 3 people how to get there. Each time ask the question in a different way.

What are 2 ways to ask someone to repeat something?

Give directions to a place in your city or town. Others have to guess the place.

Pick a *Places Around Town Card*
SING DIRECTIONS FROM YOUR SCHOOL TO THAT PLACE.

What is the most interesting tourist sight in your city or town? How do you get there from your school?

Ask a classmate for directions. After you hear them, repeat them back.

Give directions to a place in your city or town. Others have to guess the place.

the nearest bank	your favorite restaurant	the nearest gas station
the closest park	the nearest post office	the nearest drug store
the nearest bus stop	your favorite department store	your favorite supermarket
a hospital in your city or town	the nearest high school	a hotel in your city or town

- Work with a group of students.
- These people are applying for a job as a secretary. Each person does things differently.
- Talk with students in your group about which person would make the best secretary based on that person's abilities and habits.
- Explain your reasons to the class.

Barbara	Timothy	Judy	Ron	Louise
types slowly	types very quickly and accurately	sometimes types carelessly	types very well	types slowly but accurately
answers the telephone politely	answers the telephone politely	answers the telephone politely	sometimes answers the telephone impolitely	answers the telephone very softly
dresses neatly	dresses neatly	always dresses neatly	usually dresses neatly	sometimes dresses sloppily
sometimes comes to work late	often comes to work late	usually comes to work on time	comes to work early	always comes to work on time
learns new skills quickly	learns new skills slowly	learns new skills slowly	learns new skills quickly	learns new skills quickly
sometimes calls in sick	sometimes calls in sick	never calls in sick	sometimes calls in sick	rarely calls in sick

8.1 *The Best Secretary*
GROUP DISCUSSION
Side by Side Communication Games & Activity Masters 2, Page 36

- Spend 3 minutes looking very carefully at each of the following pairs of pictures.
- Put this Activity Master away and complete Activity Master 63 to see how many of these differences you can remember.

Julie	Judy	Nick	Rick
Jack	Mack	Eileen	Irene
Lenny	Benny	Mandy	Sandy
Ed	Ted	Dolly	Polly

- Circle the correct words and complete the statements below based on the illustrations on Activity Master 62.
- Look at Activity Master 62 again to check your answers. How well did you remember the differences?

1. I (can   can't) hear Julie. She speaks very _____ softly _____.

2. I (can   can't) hear Judy. She speaks very _____.

3. Rick (is   isn't) going to get a raise. He works very _____.

4. Nick (is   isn't) going to get a raise. He works very _____.

5. Mack's parents are (upset   pleased). He speaks very _____.

6. Jack's parents are (upset   pleased). He speaks very _____.

7. Eileen's boss (is   isn't) happy. She always comes to work _____.

8. Irene's boss (is   isn't) happy. She always comes to work _____.

9. (Everybody   Nobody) likes Lenny. He always plays cards _____.

10. (Everybody   Nobody) likes Benny. He always plays cards _____.

11. Mandy is a (careful   careless) driver. She drives very _____.

12. Sandy is a (careful   careless) driver. She drives very _____.

13. Ted's grandmother (is   isn't) pleased. He dresses very _____.

14. Ed's grandmother (is   isn't) pleased. He dresses very _____.

15. Donald (is   isn't) looking forward to going out with Polly this Saturday night.

    She dances very _____.

16. Ronald (is   isn't) looking forward to going out with Dolly this Saturday night.

    She dances very _____.

- Work with a partner.
- Answer the following questions about yourself. Write your answers in Column 1, using any of the words below. Be honest!
- Then talk with your partner. Before you tell your partner how you answered each question, have your partner guess what you're going to say about yourself. Write your partner's guesses in Column 2 and compare your partner's answers with yours.
- Report your answers and your partner's guesses to the class. How accurately did your partner guess?

accurately	carefully	energetically	impolitely	noisily	sloppily
attractively	carelessly	fast	loudly	politely	slowly
badly	clearly	gracefully	neatly	quietly	well
beautifully	dishonestly	honestly	nicely	rudely	

	Your Answers	Your Partner's Answers
1. How do you dress?		
2. How do you sing?		
3. How do you dance?		
4. How do you drive?		
5. How do you ski?		
6. How do you skate?		
7. How do you swim?		
8. How do you type?		
9. How do you draw?		
10. How well do you play sports?		
11. How well do you listen to people?		
12. How well do you remember things?		
13. How do you usually speak to people?		
14. How do you usually do your work?		

- Work with a partner. Don't look at your partner's paragraph.
- Your partner has information that you don't have, and you have information that your partner doesn't have.
- Ask questions about the missing information in your paragraph.
- Write the answers below. Then look at your partner's paragraph to check.

Everybody Complains About Howard

Poor Howard! Everybody always complains about him. **(1)** Howard's boss thinks _____. **(2)** She tells him _____. **(3)** His mother thinks he dresses too sloppily. **(4)** She tells him he should dress more neatly. **(5)** His upstairs neighbors think _____. **(6)** They tell him _____. **(7)** His downstairs neighbors think he goes to bed too late. **(8)** They tell him he should go to bed earlier. **(9)** His girlfriend thinks _____. **(10)** She tells him _____. **(11)** His sister thinks he drives too fast. **(12)** She tells him he should drive more slowly. **(13)** His co-workers think _____. **(14)** They tell him _____. **(15)** His grandparents think he speaks too impolitely. **(16)** They tell him he should speak more politely. **(17)** And his friends think _____. **(18)** They tell him _____. It seems that EVERYBODY complains about Howard! And what does Howard think? **(19)** He thinks everybody should stop complaining about him!

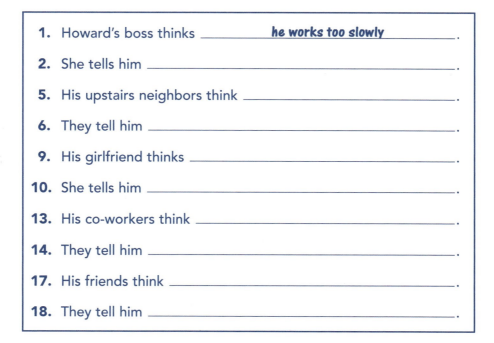

1. Howard's boss thinks _____ *he works too slowly* _____.

2. She tells him _____.

5. His upstairs neighbors think _____.

6. They tell him _____.

9. His girlfriend thinks _____.

10. She tells him _____.

13. His co-workers think _____.

14. They tell him _____.

17. His friends think _____.

18. They tell him _____.

- Work with a partner. Don't look at your partner's paragraph.
- Your partner has information that you don't have, and you have information that your partner doesn't have.
- Ask questions about the missing information in your paragraph.
- Write the answers below. Then look at your partner's paragraph to check.

Everybody Complains About Howard

Poor Howard! Everybody always complains about him. **(1)** Howard's boss thinks he works too slowly. **(2)** She tells him he should work faster. **(3)** His mother thinks _____. **(4)** She tells him _____. **(5)** His upstairs neighbors think he plays his music too loud. **(6)** They tell him he should play it more softly. **(7)** His downstairs neighbors think _____. **(8)** They tell him _____. **(9)** His girlfriend thinks he dances too awkwardly. **(10)** She tells him he should dance more gracefully. **(11)** His sister thinks _____. **(12)** She tells him _____. **(13)** His co-workers think he speaks too softly. **(14)** They tell him he should speak louder. **(15)** His grandparents think _____. **(16)** They tell him _____. **(17)** And his friends think he plays cards dishonestly. **(18)** They tell him he should play cards more honestly. It seems that EVERYBODY complains about Howard! And what does Howard think? **(19)** He thinks _____!

3. His mother thinks _____.

4. She tells him _____.

7. His downstairs neighbors think _____.

8. They tell him _____.

11. His sister thinks _____.

12. She tells him _____.

15. His grandparents think _____.

16. They tell him _____.

19. Howard thinks _____.

• Complete the following statements any way you wish, using *will* or *might*.

If you go to bed too late tonight, _____.

If you eat while you're driving, _____.

If you feel sick tomorrow, _____.

If you listen to loud music all the time, _____.

If you do your homework carelessly, _____.

If you drive too fast, _____.

If the weather is bad this weekend, _____.

If you get to work late all the time, _____.

If you sit at your desk all day, _____.

If you eat a lot of spicy food, _____.

If you don't have enough money to pay the rent, _____.

If you watch too many scary movies, _____.

If you speak impolitely to people, _____.

If you dress sloppily, _____.

If you speak too quickly, _____.

If you speak very softly, _____.

If you walk too slowly, _____.

If you don't dance very well, _____.

If you don't practice English, _____.

If you buy too many expensive things, _____.

- Put your markers on *Start.*
- Take turns tossing the Game Cube (or flipping a coin) to move your marker around the board.
- Follow the instructions in each space.

Pick an Action Card
ACT IT OUT.
_____
Everyone has to guess what you're doing.

Finish the sentence!
If I'm very hungry tonight, _____.

Pick a Consequence Card
COMPLETE IT ANY WAY YOU WANT.
_____

In 15 seconds...
tell 3 things you do very well.

START

Consequence Cards

Pick an Action Card
ACT IT OUT.
_____
Everyone has to guess what you're doing.

FINISH

Give 3 answers!
_____
You'll have bad luck if . . .

In 15 seconds...
tell 3 things you do badly.

In 15 seconds...
tell 3 things you do very quickly.

Action Cards

Pick a Consequence Card
COMPLETE IT ANY WAY YOU WANT.
_____

Pick an Action Card
ACT IT OUT.
_____
Everyone has to guess what you're doing.

In 15 seconds...
tell 3 things you do slowly.

Give 3 answers!
_____
You'll have good luck if . . .

8.6 *Adverb & Conditional Game*
BOARD GAME
Side by Side Communication Games & Activity Masters 2, Page 41

I might hurt my back if . . .	I'll get a raise if . . .	I might get a stomachache if . . .
I might get fired if . . .	My friends will be upset if . . .	I'll be very angry if . . .
I'll be very happy if . . .	I might cut myself if . . .	I'll probably get a headache if . . .
I might have an accident if . . .	My teacher will be upset if . . .	My teacher will be very happy if . . .
My boss will be very pleased if . . .	I'll have nightmares if . . .	I might hurt my eyes if . . .

driving carefully	filing slowly	typing quickly
dancing gracefully	working carelessly	playing cards dishonestly
working energetically	getting to work early	getting up late
speaking impolitely	speaking loudly	speaking softly
speaking politely	dressing neatly	dressing sloppily

- Ask other students what they were doing yesterday evening at 8 o'clock.
- When you find someone who was doing an activity on your grid, have that person write his or her name in that square.
- The first student with the most signatures wins the game.

Watching TV? Name: _____	**Reading?** Name: _____	**Playing Cards?** Name: _____
Taking a Bath? Name: _____	**Using Your Computer?** Name: _____	**Cleaning?** Name: _____
Cooking? Name: _____	**Doing Your Homework?** Name: _____	**Taking a Shower?** Name: _____
Exercising? Name: _____	**Driving Somewhere?** Name: _____	**Sleeping?** Name: _____
Listening to Music? Name: _____	**Talking on the Telephone?** Name: _____	**Visiting a Friend?** Name: _____

- What was Rob's family *doing* yesterday afternoon? What was Ron's family *doing*? Spend 3 minutes looking very carefully at these two scenes.
- Put this Activity Master aside and complete Activity Master 73 to see how many of these activities you can remember.

Rob's Family

Ron's Family

- Complete the following statements about Rob and Ron's families.
- Look at Activity Master 72 again to check your answers. How well did you remember what everybody was doing?

1. Rob's mother _____ *was reading a book* _____ .

2. Ron's mother _____ .

3. Rob's father _____ .

4. Ron's father _____ .

5. Rob's older brother _____ .

6. Ron's older brother _____ .

7. Rob's younger brother _____ .

8. Ron's younger brother _____ .

9. Rob's older sister _____ .

10. Ron's older sister _____ .

11. Rob's younger sister _____ .

12. Ron's younger sister _____ .

13. Rob's grandparents _____ .

14. Ron's grandparents _____ .

15. Rob's aunt _____ .

16. Ron's aunt _____ .

17. Rob's uncle _____ .

18. Ron's uncle _____ .

19. Rob's cousins _____ .

20. Ron's cousins _____ .

21. Rob's neighbors _____ .

22. Ron's neighbors _____ .

23. Rob _____ .

24. Ron _____ .

9.3 *I Saw You Yesterday!*
MATCHING GAME
Side by Side Communication Games & Activity Masters 2, Page 44

- A lot of unfortunate things happened to people yesterday and today! Spend 3 minutes looking very carefully at these scenes.
- Put this Activity Master aside and complete Activity Master 76 to see how many of these unfortunate things you can remember.

Yesterday

Today

- Complete the following, using these verbs:

  bite   fall   lose
  drop   get   steal
  faint   hurt   trip

- Look at Activity Master 75 again to check your answers. How many unfortunate things did you remember?

1. *Yesterday:* _____ A man hurt himself while he was fixing a door. _____

2. *Today:* _____ A woman hurt herself while she was fixing a window. _____

3. *Yesterday:* _____

4. *Today:* _____

5. *Yesterday:* _____

6. *Today:* _____

7. *Yesterday:* _____

8. *Today:* _____

9. *Yesterday:* _____

10. *Today:* _____

11. *Yesterday:* _____

12. *Today:* _____

13. *Yesterday:* _____

14. *Today:* _____

15. *Yesterday:* _____

16. *Today:* _____

17. *Yesterday:* _____

18. *Today:* _____

9.5 *A Very Bad Day!*
LISTENING GAME
Side by Side Communication Games & Activity Masters 2, Page 46

lose . . . while . . .	hurt . . . while . . .	cut . . . while . . .
drop . . . while . . .	trip . . . while . . .	fall . . . while . . .
burn . . . while . . .	faint . . . while . . .	bite . . . while . . .
poke . . . while . . .	spill . . . while . . .	steal . . . while . . .

couldn't/weren't able to	couldn't/weren't able to
have lunch with your co-workers	**watch your favorite TV program**
too busy	too tired
couldn't/weren't able to	couldn't/weren't able to
eat your lunch	**sit down on the bus**
too spicy	too crowded
couldn't/weren't able to	couldn't/weren't able to
solve the math problem	**buy the computer you wanted**
too difficult	too expensive
couldn't/weren't able to	couldn't/weren't able to
watch the science fiction movie on TV	**lift your grandfather's suitcase**
too scary	too heavy
couldn't/weren't able to	couldn't/weren't able to
get into the movie	**play on the basketball team**
too young	too short
couldn't/weren't able to	couldn't/weren't able to
go to school today	**find your cat**
too sick	too dark
couldn't/weren't able to	couldn't/weren't able to
swim in the ocean	**finish your dinner**
too cold	too full
couldn't/weren't able to	couldn't/weren't able to
ask Jennifer to go out on a date	**go sailing**
too shy	too windy
couldn't/weren't able to	couldn't/weren't able to
wear your brother's leather jacket	**sit in your friend's new chair**
too small	too uncomfortable
couldn't/weren't able to	couldn't/weren't able to
tell the police officer about the accident	**ask your boss for a raise**
too upset	too nervous

- Work with a partner. Don't look at your partner's paragraph.
- Your partner has information that you don't have, and you have information that your partner doesn't have.
- Ask questions about the missing information in your paragraph.
- Write the answers below. Then look at your partner's paragraph to check.

It was Frank's vacation last week, and there were a lot of things he wanted to do during his time off. Unfortunately, he couldn't do any of them! As a result, it was a very frustrating week. **(1)** On Monday afternoon he wanted to _____. **(2)** Unfortunately, he wasn't able to because _____. **(3)** On Tuesday evening he wanted to go to a rock concert. **(4)** Unfortunately, he couldn't do that because he had to stay home and wait for the plumber. **(5)** On Wednesday afternoon he wanted to _____. **(6)** Unfortunately, he couldn't because _____. **(7)** On Thursday evening he wanted to go to a basketball game. **(8)** However, he wasn't able to because he had to pick up his cousin at the airport. **(9)** On Friday morning he wanted to _____. **(10)** However, he wasn't able to because _____. **(11)** On Saturday evening he wanted to see a play. **(12)** Unfortunately, he couldn't because he had to fix a broken window. **(13)** And on Sunday afternoon he wanted to _____.

(14) Unfortunately, he couldn't because _____. As you can see, Frank didn't enjoy himself very much during his week off from work!

---

1. On Monday afternoon he wanted to ___*go to the beach*___.

2. He wasn't able to because _____.

5. On Wednesday afternoon he wanted to _____.

6. He couldn't because _____.

9. On Friday morning he wanted to _____.

10. He wasn't able to because _____.

13. On Sunday afternoon he wanted to _____.

14. He couldn't because _____.

- Work with a partner. Don't look at your partner's paragraph.
- Your partner has information that you don't have, and you have information that your partner doesn't have.
- Ask questions about the missing information in your paragraph.
- Write the answers below. Then look at your partner's paragraph to check.

It was also Tina's vacation last week, and there were a lot of things she wanted to do during her time off. Unfortunately, just like Frank, she couldn't do any of them! As a result, it was a terrible week for Tina. **(1)** On Monday evening she wanted to _____. **(2)** Unfortunately, she wasn't able to because _____. **(3)** On Tuesday morning she wanted to go to the zoo. **(4)** Unfortunately, she couldn't do that because she had to go to the doctor. **(5)** On Wednesday afternoon she wanted to _____. **(6)** However, she couldn't because _____. **(7)** On Thursday evening she wanted to go to the symphony. **(8)** Unfortunately, she wasn't able to because she had to fix a flat tire. **(9)** On Friday afternoon she wanted to _____. **(10)** However, she wasn't able to because _____. **(11)** On Saturday evening she wanted to go to her friend's costume party. **(12)** Unfortunately, she couldn't because she had to speak to the landlord about her broken door. **(13)** And on Sunday afternoon she wanted to _____. **(14)** Unfortunately, she couldn't because _____. As you can see, Tina didn't enjoy herself very much during her week off from work!

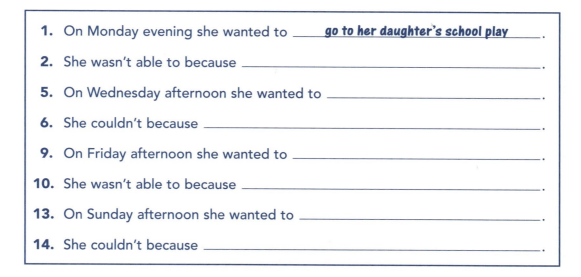

1. On Monday evening she wanted to _____ *go to her daughter's school play* _____.

2. She wasn't able to because _____.

5. On Wednesday afternoon she wanted to _____.

6. She couldn't because _____.

9. On Friday afternoon she wanted to _____.

10. She wasn't able to because _____.

13. On Sunday afternoon she wanted to _____.

14. She couldn't because _____.

- Work with a partner. Don't look at your partner's paragraph.
- Your partner has information that you don't have, and you have information that your partner doesn't have.
- Ask questions about the missing information in your paragraph.
- Write the answers below. Then look at your partner's paragraph to check.

It was Frank's vacation last week, and there were a lot of things he wanted to do during his time off. Unfortunately, he couldn't do any of them! As a result, it was a very frustrating week. **(1)** On Monday afternoon he wanted to go to the beach. **(2)** Unfortunately, he wasn't able to because he had to take his son to the doctor. **(3)** On Tuesday evening he wanted to _____. **(4)** Unfortunately, he couldn't do that because _____. **(5)** On Wednesday afternoon he wanted to attend a tennis match. **(6)** Unfortunately, he couldn't because he had to see the dentist. **(7)** On Thursday evening he wanted to _____. **(8)** However, he wasn't able to because _____. **(9)** On Friday morning he wanted to go to the museum. **(10)** However, he wasn't able to because he had to take his father to the eye doctor. **(11)** On Saturday evening he wanted to _____. **(12)** Unfortunately, he couldn't because _____. **(13)** And on Sunday afternoon he wanted to go to a baseball game. **(14)** Unfortunately, he couldn't because he had to take his dog to the vet. As you can see, Frank didn't enjoy himself very much during his week off from work!

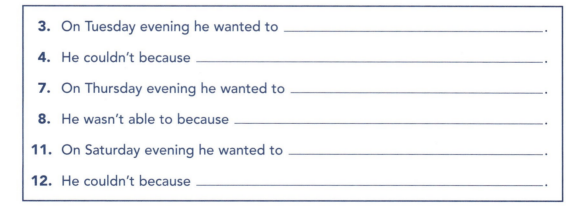

3. On Tuesday evening he wanted to _____.

4. He couldn't because _____.

7. On Thursday evening he wanted to _____.

8. He wasn't able to because _____.

11. On Saturday evening he wanted to _____.

12. He couldn't because _____.

- Work with a partner. Don't look at your partner's paragraph.
- Your partner has information that you don't have, and you have information that your partner doesn't have.
- Ask questions about the missing information in your paragraph.
- Write the answers below. Then look at your partner's paragraph to check.

It was also Tina's vacation last week, and there were a lot of things she wanted to do during her time off. Unfortunately, just like Frank, she couldn't do any of them! As a result, it was a terrible week for Tina. **(1)** On Monday evening she wanted to go to her daughter's school play. **(2)** Unfortunately, she wasn't able to because she had to baby-sit for her neighbor. **(3)** On Tuesday morning she wanted to _____.

(4) Unfortunately, she couldn't do that because _____. **(5)** On Wednesday afternoon she wanted to go to a soccer game. **(6)** However, she couldn't because she had to drive her daughter to her ballet lesson. **(7)** On Thursday evening she wanted to _____. **(8)** Unfortunately, she wasn't able to because _____.

(9) On Friday afternoon she wanted to go to her neighbor's birthday party.

(10) However, she wasn't able to because she had to meet with her son's teacher.

(11) On Saturday evening she wanted to _____. **(12)** Unfortunately, she couldn't because _____. **(13)** And on Sunday afternoon she wanted to go to the park.

(14) Unfortunately, she couldn't because she had to visit her boss in the hospital. As you can see, Tina didn't enjoy herself very much during her week off from work!

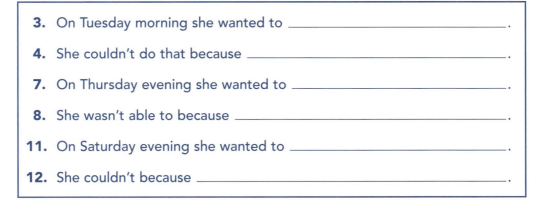

3. On Tuesday morning she wanted to _____.

4. She couldn't do that because _____.

7. On Thursday evening she wanted to _____.

8. She wasn't able to because _____.

11. On Saturday evening she wanted to _____.

12. She couldn't because _____.

- Ask other students, "Do you have to _____ this week?"
- When you find someone who has got to do an activity on your grid, have that person write his or her name in that square.
- The first student with the most signatures wins the game.

Go to the Bank? Name: _____	**Buy Food at the Supermarket?** Name: _____	**Go to the Doctor?** Name: _____
Pay Bills? Name: _____	**Wash the Dishes?** Name: _____	**Work?** Name: _____
Fix Something? Name: _____	**Attend a Meeting?** Name: _____	**Do the Laundry?** Name: _____
Make Dinner? Name: _____	**Baby-sit?** Name: _____	**Study?** Name: _____
Help a Friend? Name: _____	**Clean Your House or Apartment?** Name: _____	**Feed the Dog?** Name: _____

Ability & Obligations Game

85

- Put your markers on *Start*.
- Take turns tossing the *Game Cube* (or flipping a coin) to move your marker around the board.
- Follow the instructions in each space.

START

Tell something you couldn't do last week and give the reason.

? Tell something a classmate wasn't able to do last week. Then ask the classmate: "Is that true?"

In 15 seconds... tell 3 things you weren't able to do when you were very young.

? What are 3 ways to say you "have to" study tonight?

In 15 seconds... tell 3 things you had to do last week.

Roll the Ability Cube APOLOGIZE TO A CLASSMATE USING THE WORD OR EXPRESSION ON THE CUBE.

In 15 seconds... tell 3 things you've got to do next week.

You won't be able to help a friend this week. Apologize to your friend and give a very good reason.

Roll the Ability Cube APOLOGIZE TO A CLASSMATE USING THE WORD OR EXPRESSION ON THE CUBE.

Complete the following. Sing your answer!
I couldn't _____.
I was too _____.

? You went somewhere recently and enjoyed yourself. Where did you go? Why did you enjoy yourself?

? Your friend won't be able to help you do something. What do you say to your friend?

FINISH

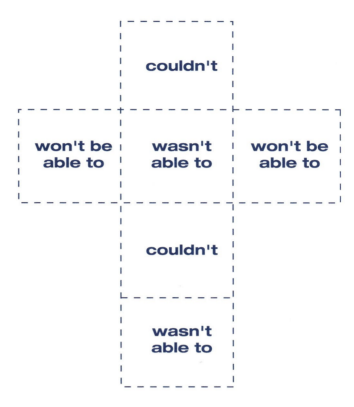

11.1 *A Complete Checkup*
LISTENING GRID
11.2 *Medical Checkup Pantomime*
PANTOMIME GAME
Side by Side Communication Games & Activity Masters 2, Pages 52, 53

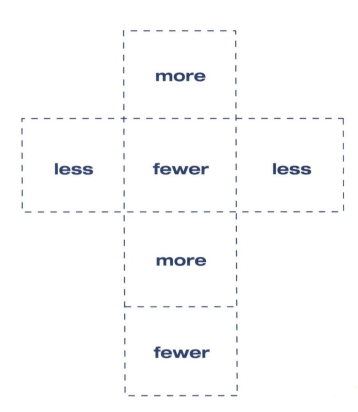

- Make up rules using *must* and *mustn't* for a business, an apartment building, and a school.
- Present your rules to the class.

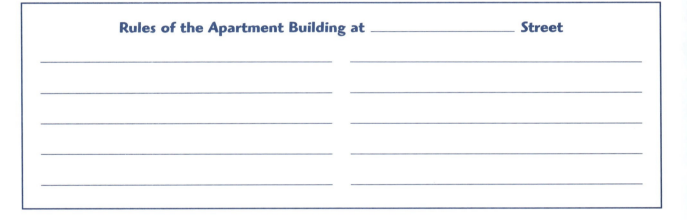

Rules of the "_____" Company

_____

_____

_____

_____

_____

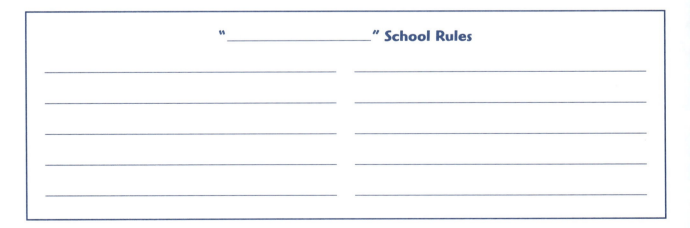

Rules of the Apartment Building at _____ Street

_____

_____

_____

_____

_____

"_____" School Rules

_____

_____

_____

_____

_____

- Work with a group of students.
- Talk with each other until you agree on two things a person *should* do in each of the following situations and one thing a person definitely *mustn't* do.
- Complete the following and then share your conclusions with the class.

1. If you want to get a promotion at work, . . .

you should _____.

you should _____.

and you mustn't _____.

2. If you want to do well in English class, . . .

you should _____.

you should _____.

and you mustn't _____.

3. If you want to save a lot of money, . . .

you should _____.

you should _____.

and you mustn't _____.

4. If you want to have a very clean house or apartment, . . .

you should _____.

you should _____.

and you mustn't _____.

5. If you want to always be healthy and happy, . . .

you should _____.

you should _____.

and you mustn't _____.

Health & Advice Game

- Put your markers on *Start*.
- Take turns tossing the Game Cube (or flipping a coin) to move your marker around the board.
- Follow the instructions in each space.

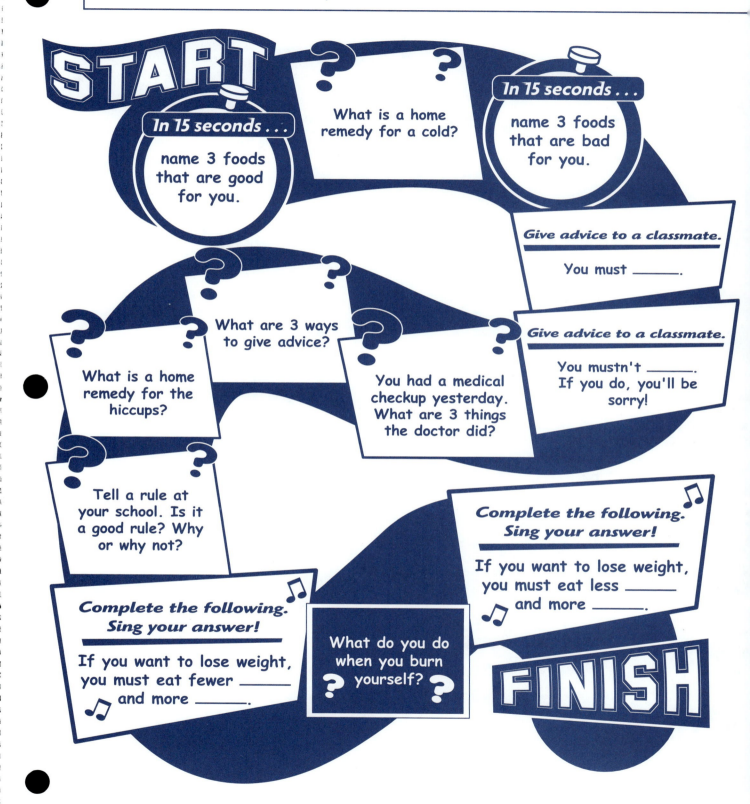

START

In 15 seconds . . .
name 3 foods that are good for you.

What is a home remedy for a cold?

In 15 seconds . . .
name 3 foods that are bad for you.

Give advice to a classmate.
You must _____.

What are 3 ways to give advice?

Give advice to a classmate.
You mustn't _____.
If you do, you'll be sorry!

What is a home remedy for the hiccups?

You had a medical checkup yesterday. What are 3 things the doctor did?

Tell a rule at your school. Is it a good rule? Why or why not?

Complete the following. Sing your answer!
If you want to lose weight, you must eat less _____ and more _____.

Complete the following. Sing your answer!
If you want to lose weight, you must eat fewer _____ and more _____.

What do you do when you burn yourself?

FINISH

- Ask other students what they will be doing this evening at 8 o'clock.
- When you find someone who is going to be doing an activity on your grid, have that person write his or her name in that square.
- The first student with the most signatures wins the game.

Reading? Name: _____	**Exercising?** Name: _____	**Paying Bills?** Name: _____
Studying? Name: _____	**Having Dinner in a Restaurant?** Name: _____	**Listening to Music?** Name: _____
Playing Cards? Name: _____	**Visiting a Friend?** Name: _____	**Shopping?** Name: _____
Cleaning? Name: _____	**Seeing a Movie in a Movie Theater?** Name: _____	**Chatting Online?** Name: _____
Working? Name: _____	**Taking a Bath?** Name: _____	**Watching TV?** Name: _____

- Work with a partner. (Don't show this schedule to your partner.)
- Ask your partner questions about what Betty will be doing this week.
- Write the answers in the schedule below.
- Compare schedules with your partner.

Schedule for the Week

Monday   *Morning*   *Afternoon*

meet with a client

Tuesday   *Morning*   *Afternoon*

attend a meeting

Wednesday   *Morning*   *Afternoon*

drive to the airport

Thursday   *Morning*   *Afternoon*

speak to my lawyer

Friday   *Morning*   *Afternoon*

have a medical checkup

Saturday   *Morning*   *Afternoon*

rearrange furniture

Sunday   *Morning*   *Afternoon*

hook up my VCR

- Work with a partner. (Don't show this schedule to your partner.)
- Ask your partner questions about what Betty will be doing this week.
- Write the answers in the schedule below.
- Compare schedules with your partner.

Schedule for the Week

Monday   *Morning*   *Afternoon*

_____   **prepare a report**

Tuesday   *Morning*   *Afternoon*

write e-mails _____

Wednesday   *Morning*   *Afternoon*

_____   **fly to Toronto**

Thursday   *Morning*   *Afternoon*

return from Toronto _____

Friday   *Morning*   *Afternoon*

_____   **see the dentist**

Saturday   *Morning*   *Afternoon*

move to my new apartment _____

Sunday   *Morning*   *Afternoon*

_____   **exercise at my health club**

- Work with a partner. (Don't show this diagram to your partner.) You also each have a set of *Tomorrow Action Cards.*
- Partner A chooses two or more *Action Cards* and places them in each part of the day.
- Partner B asks Yes/No questions in order to find out what Partner A will be doing during each part of the day, then arranges the cards on his or her diagram based on the answers.
- Compare with your partner's diagram to see if your cards are in the same parts of the day.
- Then switch roles. Partner B chooses the cards and Partner A asks the questions.

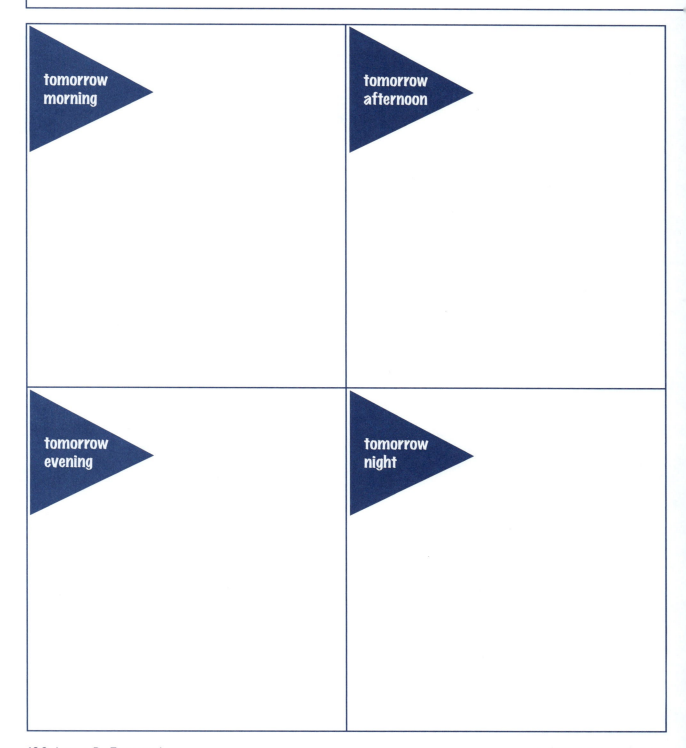

tomorrow morning

tomorrow afternoon

tomorrow evening

tomorrow night

12.3 *Lots to Do Tomorrow!*
LISTENING GAME
Side by Side Communication Games & Activity Masters 2, Page 60

12.3 *Lots to Do Tomorrow!*
LISTENING GAME
Side by Side Communication Games & Activity Masters 2, Page 60

- Put your markers on *Start.*
- Take turns tossing the *Game Cube* (or flipping a coin) to move your marker around the board.
- Follow the instructions in each space.

In 15 seconds . . .
tell 3 things you'll be doing next year.

START

FINISH

Tell something you'll be doing soon that you're looking forward to.

Complete the following:
I'll be _____ing until _____.
Then ask your classmates, "Do you think that's true?"

What will you be doing tonight at 8 o'clock?
Draw your answer.
Everyone has to guess what you'll be doing.

Sing to a classmate:
You'll be _____ing until _____!
Then ask the classmate: "Is that true?"

Key Word Cards

Pick a Key Word Card
ASK A QUESTION: "HOW MUCH LONGER _____?" USING THE WORD ON THE CARD.

Make up a message for your telephone answering machine.

Complete the following:
I'll be _____ing for _____.
Then ask your classmates, "Do you think that's true?"

Pick a Key Word Card
ASK A QUESTION: "HOW MUCH LONGER _____?" USING THE WORD ON THE CARD.

Tell something you'll be doing soon that you *aren't* looking forward to.

Complete the following:
I'll be taking English classes until _____.

You're calling your friend Alex on the phone, but Alex isn't there. What do you say to the person who answers?

the floor	furniture	bills	the newspaper
letters	your shirts	your dog	mittens
TV	a bath	to music	cards
the piano	online	the kitchen	your garage
cookies	your homework	videos	to the radio
your front door	flowers	the cat	pictures
your exercises	your rugs	English	a shower

- Spend 3 minutes looking very carefully at each of the following pairs of pictures.
- Put this Activity Master aside and complete Activity Master 100 to see how many of these differences you can remember.

13.1 *What Are the Differences?*
MEMORY GAME
Side by Side Communication Games & Activity Masters 2, Page 62

- Complete the following conversations, using pronouns and these words in your answers.

burn	get	spill
call	lose	visit
cut	poke	

- Look at Activity Master 99 again to check your answers. How much did you remember?

1. A. Did Sam and Susan really lose their watches yesterday?

   B. Yes. _____ **He lost his in the park, and she lost hers at the beach.** _____

2. A. Is it true that you and your cousins lost your headphones yesterday?

   B. Yes. _____

3. A. How often do you and your grandmother call each other?

   B. _____

4. A. I know that you and your husband speak to your son in college every week. How often do you call each other?

   B. _____

5. A. How often do you and your relatives in Miami visit each other?

   B. _____

6. A. How often do you and your wife and aunt in Cleveland visit each other?

   B. _____

7. A. What happened to Charlie and his wife today?

   B. _____

8. A. What happened to you and your children this morning?

   B. _____

9. A. Did you hear what happened to me and my sister yesterday afternoon?

   B. Yes. _____

10. A. Yesterday was a terrible day for my wife and me and for our friends.

    B. Yes. I heard. _____

13.2 *Bob's Bad Night!*
TELL-A-STORY
Side by Side Communication Games & Activity Masters 2, Page 63

Is there anything red in your classroom? What is it?	Say something nice about a classmate.	Can you recommend anything for a headache? What do you recommend?	Is anyone in your family very talented? Who is it? What does he or she do?
What is something that's unhealthy for you?	Tell something that tastes good.	Does anybody in your class know how to skate? Ask!	Can you cook anything that's delicious? What is it?
Is there anything green in your classroom? What is it?	You found someone's watch. What are you going to do?	Can anyone in your class fix a car? Ask!	What is something someone gave you for a present?
There's something wrong with your CD player. What are you going to do?	Do you need anything from the supermarket? What do you need?	Tell something nice that someone did recently.	Tell something you do very well.
What is something that's very expensive?	Recommend someone who can fix a sink.	What is something you can do in the summer but you can't do in the winter?	Say something very slowly!
Do you know anybody who can sing beautifully? Who is it?	Someone told you some bad news. What do you say to that person?	Tell something you have to do tomorrow.	What is something you'll be doing in ten years that you aren't doing now?
You're lost! Ask someone for directions.	Are you going to do anything exciting this weekend? Tell about it.	Give somebody a warning. Tell the person what might happen.	What is something that's very fancy?

13.3 *Some & Any Question Game*
TEAM COMPETITION
Side by Side Communication Games & Activity Masters 2, Page 64

Is there anything blue in your classroom? What is it?	Say something nice about a member of your family.	Can you recommend anything for a sore throat? What do you recommend?	Is anybody in your family a very interesting person? Who is it? Why is he or she interesting?
What is something that's healthy for you?	Tell something that tastes terrible.	Does anybody in your class know how to ski? Ask!	Can you cook anything that's delicious? What is it?
Is there anything yellow in your classroom? What is it?	You found someone's cell phone. What are you going to do?	Can anyone in your class fix a computer? Ask!	What is something you gave someone for a present?
There's something wrong with your TV. What are you going to do?	Do you need anything from the drug store? What do you need?	Tell something bad that someone did recently.	Tell something you do badly.
What is something that isn't very expensive?	Recommend someone who can fix a broken fence.	What is something you can do in the winter but you can't do in the summer?	Say something very quickly!
Do you know anybody who can dance gracefully? Who is it?	Someone told you some good news. What do you say to that person?	Tell something you have to do this weekend.	What is something you were doing ten years ago that you aren't doing now?
You're lost! Ask someone for directions.	Did you do anything exciting last weekend? Tell about it.	Give somebody a warning. Tell the person what might happen.	What is something that's very soft?

Notes

Notes

Game Index

Game Index

Board Games

3.7 The Food Game
5.2 Let's Compare! Game
6.1 Superlative Game
7.5 Getting Around Town Game
8.6 Adverb & Conditional Game
10.4 Ability & Obligations Game
11.6 Health & Advice Game
12.4 Future Continuous Game

Classroom Search Games

1.1 What Do You Like to Do?
9.1 What Were You Doing?
10.3 Things They've Got to Do
12.1 What Will You Be Doing?

Group Discussion

5.6 Good Advice
8.1 The Best Secretary
11.5 We've Got Some Advice for You

Group Project

6.3 Commercial Competition
11.4 Make the Rules!

Guessing Games

8.5 What's the Consequence?
10.1 Guess the Situation!

Information Gaps

3.3 My Shopping List
3.5 Sam's Supermarket
4.3 Debbie Can't Decide
7.2 How Do I Get There?
12.2 Betty's Busy Week

Interviews

4.4 I Can't Decide
5.4 What Do You Think?
8.3 How Do You Do Things?

Listening Games

1.3 The Mills Family Yesterday & Tomorrow
2.2 The Foods in My Kitchen
7.4 Let's Go By Bus!
12.3 Lots to Do Tomorrow!

Listening Grids

1.2 What Do They Like to Do?
3.1 Foods I Need at the Supermarket
7.3 Mystery Places
9.5 A Very Bad Day!
11.1 A Complete Checkup

Matching Games

2.5 What Did You Buy at the Supermarket?
7.1 Good Directions!/Wrong Directions!
9.3 I Saw You Yesterday!

Memory Games

2.4 The Foods at Amy's Party
3.4 The Foods in Kevin's Kitchen
5.5 Can You Remember?
8.2 How Well Do You Remember?
9.2 Doing Different Things
9.4 What Happened to These People?
13.1 What Are the Differences?

Mystery Games

4.1 What's My Future?
4.2 Frieda, the Fortune Teller

Pair Discussion

5.1 Comparatively Speaking
5.3 Which Do You Prefer?

Pantomime Games

9.6 Guess What Happened to Me!
11.2 Medical Checkup Pantomime

Pick-a-Card

2.1 Go Shopping!
3.2 Go Shopping!

Picture Differences

2.3 What's the Same & What's Different About These Kitchens?

Story Games

1.4 Happy Birthday!

3.6 A Wonderful Dinner

4.5 George, the Pessimist!

6.2 Ray & Roy: Two Very Different Brothers

8.4 Everybody Complains About Howard

10.2 Frank and Tina: Two Unlucky People

Team Competition

11.3 If You Want to Lose Weight

13.3 Some & Any Question Game

Tell-a-Story

13.2 Bob's Bad Night!